THE MTSS START-UP GUIDE

Jessica Djabrayan Hannigan

John E. Hannigan

THE MTSS START-UP GUIDE

Ensuring Equity, Access, and Inclusivity for ALL Students

FOR INFORMATION:

Corwin

A SAGE Company

2455 Teller Road

Thousand Oaks, California 91320

(800) 233-9936

www.corwin.com

SAGE Publications Ltd.

1 Oliver's Yard

55 City Road

London EC1Y 1SP

United Kingdom

SAGE Publications India Pvt. Ltd.

B 1/I 1 Mohan Cooperative Industrial Area

Mathura Road, New Delhi 110 044

India

SAGE Publications Asia-Pacific Pte. Ltd.

18 Cross Street #10-10/11/12

China Square Central

Singapore 048423

Publisher: Jessica Allan

Senior Content Development Editor: Lucas Schleicher

Associate Content Development Editor: Mia Rodriguez

Production Editor: Tori Mirsadjadi

Copy Editor: Shamila Swamy, QuADS Prepress (P) Ltd.

Typesetter: C&M Digitals (P) Ltd.

Proofreader: Dennis Webb

Indexer: Integra

Cover Designer: Gail Buschman

Marketing Manager: Maura Sullivan

Library of Congress Cataloging-in-Publication Data

Names: Djabrayan Hannigan, Jessica, author. | Hannigan, John E., author.

Title: The MTSS start-up guide : ensuring equity, access, and inclusivity for ALL students / Jessica Djabrayan Hannigan and John E. Hannigan.

Description: Los Angeles : Corwin, [2021] | Includes bibliographical references and index.

Identifiers: LCCN 2020022969 | ISBN 9781544394244 (paperback) | ISBN 9781544394282 (epub) | ISBN 9781544394251 (epub) | ISBN 9781544394268 (pdf)

Subjects: LCSH: Student assistance programs—United States—Handbooks, manuals, etc. | Student assistance programs—United States—Case studies. | Academic achievement—United States. | School improvement programs—United States. | Educational equalization—United States.

Classification: LCC LB3430.5 .D53 2021 | DDC 371.4—dc23

LC record available at https://lccn.loc.gov/2020022969

This book is printed on acid-free paper.

21 22 23 24 10 9 8 7 6 5 4 3

CONTENTS

Preface   vii

Publisher's Acknowledgments   viii

About the Authors   ix

PART I: WHAT AND WHY OF MTSS   1

Chapter 1. What and Why of MTSS   2

PART II: MTSS IN PRACTICE   7

Chapter 2. Frequently Asked Questions From the Field   8

Chapter 3. MTSS School Case Study Scenarios   12

    Scenario 1: MTSS in Everything Everything School   12

    Scenario 2: MTSS in a District-Led School   12

    Scenario 3: MTSS in a Site-Led School   13

PART III: WHERE DO WE START?   15

Chapter 4. Assessing Your MTSS Readiness and Current State   16

    What Is the MTSS Readiness Screener?   16

    Who Should Complete the MTSS Readiness Screener?   17

    What Is the MTSS Start-Up Assessment?   18

    Who Should Complete the MTSS Start-Up Assessment? 18

Chapter 5. MTSS Start-Up Guide: A Blueprint for Start-Up Implementation   23

    How Best to Utilize This Section of the Chapter   24

    Indicator 1   25

    Indicator 2   30

    Indicator 3   40

    Indicator 4   52

    Indicator 5   58

    Indicator 6   63

    Indicator 7   74

    Indicator 8   80

    Indicator 9   83

    Indicator 10   87

PART IV: BRINGING IT ALL TOGETHER   93

Chapter 6. Bringing It All Together   94

References   97
Index   98

 Visit the companion website at
resources.corwin.com/MTSSStartupGuide
for downloadable resources.

PREFACE

This book is designed to guide readers through an interactive process to understand the why, what, and how of effective implementation of Multi-Tiered Systems of Support as they begin this work in their school. Specifically, readers will learn how to audit, align, and coordinate their current practices, structures, interventions, and resources across all academic and social well-being areas of an educational system in order to support *all* students. Readers will also learn how to effectively integrate data-based decision-making and a continuous school improvement lens to regularly monitor the effectiveness of implementation. Readers will gain access to a blueprint start-up guide that will help them begin the work necessary to create an infrastructure to improve equity, access, and inclusivity for *all* students in their school.

PUBLISHER'S ACKNOWLEDGMENTS

Corwin gratefully acknowledges the contributions of the following reviewers:

Jo-Anne Goldberg, LCSW-EdS
Director of Special Education
Mainland Regional High School
Linwood, New Jersey

Whitney Schexnider
Statewide Instructional Coordinator
Boise State University
Boise, Idaho

ABOUT THE AUTHORS

Dr. Jessica Djabrayan Hannigan is an assistant professor in the educational leadership department at California State University, Fresno. She works with schools and districts throughout the nation on designing and implementing effective behavior systems. Her expertise includes Response to Intervention Behavior, Multi-Tiered Systems of Support, Positive Behavior Interventions and Supports, Social and Emotional Learning, and more. The combination of her special education and student support services background and school- and district-level administration and higher education research experiences has allowed her to develop inclusive, research-based best practices around systemic implementation of behavior initiatives throughout the nation. Some of her recognitions include being named California Outstanding School Psychologist of the Year and Administrator of the Year, receiving the Outstanding Faculty Publications and Service Award, being recognized by the California Legislature Assembly for her work in social justice and equity, and receiving the inaugural Association of California School Administrators Exemplary Woman in Education Award in 2017 for her relentless work around equity in schools.

John Hannigan, EdD, is an executive leadership coach for Fresno County Superintendent of Schools in California. He has served in education for over 17 years as a principal, assistant principal, instructional coach, and teacher. Under his leadership, his school has received numerous awards and recognitions, including California State Distinguished School, Gold Ribbon School, Title I Academic School, Positive Behavioral Interventions and Supports (Platinum Level), and an exemplary Response to Intervention school for both academics and behavior. His school was selected as a knowledge development site for the statewide scaling up of Multi-Tiered Systems of Support.

PART I

WHAT AND WHY OF MTSS

CHAPTER 1

WHAT AND WHY OF MTSS

THE WHAT: MTSS, a framework that provides schools with structures for designing multi-tiered systems of support and the alignment of resources across all areas of academic and social well-being.

THE WHY: Equity, access, and inclusivity for *all* students; current state of implementation; and implementation challenges

In order to know what it is you are beginning to implement, you need to define Multi-Tiered Systems of Support (MTSS), its purpose, and the roles and responsibilities of all the stakeholders involved to make implementation a success. We relate the MTSS work to both organizational theory and improvement science components; in short, we provide a process to ensure that implementation is working and ways to identify where to improve/address barriers in implementation. According to Bolman and Deal (2007), in their book *Reframing Organizations: Artistry, Choice, and Leadership*, organizational theory refers to a set of interrelated concepts and definitions that explain the behavior of individuals, groups, or subgroups who interact with one another to perform activities intended toward the accomplishment of a common goal.

In their book, Bolman and Deal (2007) depict the results of an organization when stakeholders are working in silos. They share an example from 9/11 about the courageous police officers and firefighters. In short, they explain how both groups responded to the serious crisis and did their jobs exactly as they were trained to. But the authors also highlight that, unfortunately, the two groups approached that crisis in silos at first because there was not enough time during the crisis to really coordinate, align, and work together to respond to it. We see at times this type of misalignment and mis-coordination of work/resources within schools as we coordinate efforts to support students (e.g., an English learner development teacher who will pull out and work with English learners, the special education [SPED] teacher who only works with students on an Individualized Education Program, or the school psychologist whose job is only testing for SPED), rather than a collective and coordinated effort to support *all* students while utilizing the expertise of the entire staff.

We wrote this book to help you *start the work* of MTSS implementation correctly and with ease, rather than following a fill-in-the-blanks approach later. The design of this book is simple. You will begin with an audit of the entire MTSS (readiness and assessment system). This will allow you to take an honest look at your current state of implementation. After you complete that component, you will read about the beginning start-up indicators of MTSS implementation and fill in any component of your readiness or current state audit that needs work. The book will end with additional information on how to utilize the elements of continuous school improvement to ensure that what you are doing is working throughout. Remember this is a start-up guide!

As former school site leaders, we were once in this exact position—the very beginning of establishing MTSS work. We first needed to know what the definition of MTSS even was. How is it different from what we currently had in place with Response to Intervention (RTI)? We work with schools and districts throughout the nation, so we wanted to have a general definition that captured the essence overall. Before we provide the definition we derived based on our investigation of the various definitions of MTSS in each state department of education across the United States, we want you to examine what your current definition of MTSS is, including the key components, and what you think the purpose of MTSS implementation is. Come back to your definition after you have read the next section, and finally write down what your operational definition will be at your school or district so everyone implementing MTSS is starting with the same definition. How does this definition align with your school's mission/vision (your school's fundamental purpose and what it aspires to become)? This is really important because if the stakeholders do not know the *why* of the implementation, the *what* does not really matter. Every policy, practice, and support for academics and social well-being should be scrutinized by the school leadership to align with your mission/vision and with schoolwide MTSS goals.

Define MTSS.

_____

_____

_____

What are the key components of MTSS?

_____

_____

What is the purpose of implementing MTSS at your school?

_____

_____

_____

Write your school's operational definition of MTSS and the purpose of implementing it here.

_____

_____

_____

_____

Come back to the last prompt after you have read the next section to see how you did and write the operational definition of what MTSS is or will be at your school. *Note:* You may have a definition defined by your district or state level; that is fine, write that down. The important thing here is that you all are consistently defining what it even is that you are implementing and why it is necessary to do so.

Also, understand that an acronym is not going to fix or improve a school; the actual implementation and understanding of what we are doing to work together to improve the school, and why, are going to give you the outcomes that are best for your students and adults.

What did we find in our investigation of MTSS in all the state department of education definitions? To be honest, we found every version of a combination of or a rebranding of RTI at Work, Professional Learning Communities (PLC) at Work, Positive Behavior Interventions and Supports (PBIS), Social and Emotional Learning (SEL), and Universal Design for Learning (UDL). In a way this was a relief to us because we always believed that MTSS was interchangeable with what RTI was designed to be when implemented with true fidelity and that it wasn't an entirely new concept. Although this book is not a replacement for trainings in any of these frameworks, it is designed to help you get started in this work. If you are interested in the best-practice work of RTI and PLC, we strongly recommend the books *Taking Action*, *Learning by Doing*, and *Behavior Solutions*; for SEL or behavior systems work, we recommend the CASEL website (https:// casel.org/), PBIS Tier 1, Tier 2, and Tier 3 handbooks, and *Building Behavior* as your deep dive for these content areas. So, based on our investigation of the definition of MTSS and our shared experiences working with schools throughout the nation, we have synthesized this work into a universal MTSS Model that encompasses the commonalities of the key evidence indicators utilized in the various state frameworks across the county.

This MTSS Model is defined as a systemic framework that requires the alignment and coordination of all the structures, conditions, and supports in place for designing levels or tiers of *prevention (all)*, *intervention (some)*, and *remediation (few)* for both academics and social well-being based on student data. The goal of implementing MTSS in this fashion is to create a school designed to serve the "whole child." The primary focus is on *equity, inclusivity, and access* for all students, with the shared ownership and collaboration of all stakeholders (i.e., students, teachers, staff, administrators, families, the community, policy makers and lawmakers, partnerships, etc.).

The MTSS Start-Up Guide is designed to provide an evidence indicator–oriented framework and success criteria for each of the 10 indicators identified.

This book identifies and describes the MTSS start-up indicators and success criteria, explains how to assess your system's current state relative to each indicator, and provides some practitioner tools and tips to start MTSS implementation. To build a strong implementation of MTSS in your school, the following 10 essential indicators must be in place.

The 10 Indicators of MTSS Implementation

1		**Indicator 1:** Establish an MTSS team (i.e., team-driven and shared leadership).
2		**Indicator 2:** Assess stakeholder beliefs, perceptions, shared values, and identity, and establish the mission and purpose of the MTSS team and all stakeholders (i.e., families, school, community, partnerships, etc.).
3		**Indicator 3:** Establish and apportion roles and responsibilities among MTSS team members and all stakeholders (i.e., shared ownership and responsibility).
4		**Indicator 4:** Audit current organizational structures and evidence-based practices (i.e., tiered processes/continuum of supports in place, programs, teams, human resources/expertise/training, initiatives, interventions) for academics and behavior.
5		**Indicator 5:** Assess the current state of academic and behavior instruction based on multiple data points (i.e., data-based problem-solving and decision-making).
6		**Indicator 6:** Develop and share MTSS SMART* goals and actions for academics and behavior (i.e., based on assessment, screener, trend, qualitative, and quantitative data).
7		**Indicator 7:** Set up a progress-monitoring system/benchmarks for MTSS, and ensure that assessment and data are up-to-date and available for decision-making.
8		**Indicator 8:** Set up clear communication structures between the MTSS team and all stakeholders.
9		**Indicator 9:** Set up ongoing MTSS professional learning for all stakeholders.
10		**Indicator 10:** Set up a process for ongoing evaluation and continuous improvement of MTSS implementation effectiveness and fidelity.

Icon Source: istock.com/appleuzr

*Note: SMART refers to specific, measurable, achievable, realistic, and timely.

Before you delve into these 10 indicators with your team, it is important for you to know some frequently asked questions from the field, acquaint yourself with common MTSS implementation start-up scenarios, and audit your current state.

What am I thinking about at this stage in the book?

PART II

MTSS IN PRACTICE

CHAPTER 2

FREQUENTLY ASKED QUESTIONS FROM THE FIELD

Everything used in this start-up guide is based on the needs of the educators we worked with in the initial stages of MTSS implementation. This book is written by practitioners for practitioners. Here are the most frequently asked questions from the field:

1. **What does MTSS stand for?**

   Multi-Tiered Systems of Supports

2. **What is the significant difference between PBIS and MTSS?**

   PBIS is a multi-tiered framework to support students with their behavior. MTSS aligns the entire system of supports for academics *and* behavior (social well-being). MTSS is inclusive of various behavior initiatives (i.e., SEL, restorative practices, trauma-informed practices, character education, culturally responsive teaching, etc.), one of which is also PBIS.

3. **Specifically, what is different when schools that already have PBIS implemented begin the work of MTSS?**

   These schools would have an advantage because they would currently have a behavior team already in place to look at data to make decisions on the behavior systems on their campus in each tier. MTSS would create the same process to support academic supports on their campus. MTSS would also help align the work between academic and social supports at the school, focusing on the needs of the whole child.

4. **What is the difference between MTSS and RTI?**

   Among the key similarities described in most descriptions of MTSS and RTI, is that both rely on RTI data gathering through universal screening, data-driven decision-making, and problem-solving teams, and are focused on the Common Core State Standards. However, most states define the MTSS process as having a broader approach than RTI, addressing the needs of all students by aligning the entire system of initiatives, supports, and resources and by implementing continuous-improvement processes at all levels of the system. We would argue that any model RTI school would also have such structures firmly in place for both academics and behavior; for this reason, we use "RTI" and "MTSS" interchangeably.

   As we support schools across the country, we are faced with many districts, and even state departments of education, treating "RTI" as a bad word, instead of taking an honest look at the lack of understanding, misconceptions, and implementation errors. We've heard, "Whatever you do, don't call it RTI; we call it MTSS now" or "RTI is a bad word in our state, and Tier III is only for SPED." We can go on and on with a long list of misconceptions. Based on this comparison example, it is clear there is a disconnect with and misunderstanding of the core components of RTI, which has led to this progression of rebranding the terms from "RTI" to "MTSS."

Simply put, if you are currently implementing RTI well, you are implementing MTSS. Don't communicate to your staff that you are changing gears and implementing a new framework.

5. **How is UDL connected to MTSS?**

   UDL is a best-practice approach in Tier 1 classroom design for instruction. It takes into consideration the variability in learning, so lessons are designed with this in mind. This is all part of Tier 1 prevention.

   The teacher understands and implements the three areas of UDL in the classroom: (1) engagement (the *why* of learning—interest and motivation are stimulated with the lessons being taught), (2) representation (the *what* of learning—information is presented in different ways, multiple modalities), and (3) action and expression (the *how* of learning—students can demonstrate what they have learned or know in different ways).

6. **Is PBIS the only approach that should be implemented in MTSS?**

   Absolutely not. The initial MTSS models dating back to 2011 created a Venn diagram of sorts, blending both RTI and PBIS to create MTSS and to reduce duplication of training and practices as MTSS was a new model.

   While PBIS does lend itself to being closer aligned to a three-tier model than other behavior initiatives, it is certainly necessary to have staff build resilience and growth mindsets, have and hold high expectations for all students, recognize the importance of including students' cultural references in all aspects of learning, and create a place where students are empowered to have a voice in their learning (culturally responsive teaching), while understanding the importance of providing a safe, informed, and understanding learning environment for students who have experienced adverse childhood experiences. Such an environment helps staff recognize the signs and symptoms of trauma in a student and actively prevent retraumatization, while teaching emotional regulation skills (trauma-informed practices)—a place where we shift our mindset about discipline from punitive to restorative, to improve relationships and remedy and learn from injustices (restorative justice). Behavior initiatives should not be in competition with one another; all of the above listed are important (in addition to SEL and character education) for a healthy school culture.

7. **How does one explain the difference that Tier 3 is not synonymous with SPED?**

   The RTI at Work model, developed by Mattos and Buffum (2015), was the first to visualize the RTI at Work pyramid as inverted. Many states, districts, and schools have mistakenly viewed RTI as a pathway to SPED identification. This misinterpretation gets visually reinforced when SPED is placed at the apex of the pyramid and it becomes "steps to take" or another "box to check" to qualify a student for SPED. However, the inverted pyramid represents a school's focus on each student's individual needs. The tiers must be viewed as the targeted levels of support a school must provide to ensure that all students learn at high levels; in doing so, a secondary benefit of effective RTI implementation is that educators can identify students who do not respond to targeted levels of support and may have a specific learning disability.

> RTI's underlying premise is that schools should not delay providing help for struggling students until they fall far enough behind to qualify for SPED, but instead should provide timely, targeted, systematic interventions to all students who demonstrate the need. (Buffum et al., 2012, p. xiii)

8. **Where does Gifted and Talented Education or enrichment fit in MTSS?**

   MTSS is a framework designed to support the needs of the whole child. So if the needs of some are for extension opportunities, then that is what should be provided. Educators oftentimes confuse the terms "enrichment" and "extension." To understand their difference, it is critical that these terms are commonly defined and become part of your MTSS schoolwide team discussions and planning.

   For example, if intervention in MTSS answers the question "How do we respond when students haven't learned?", then extension is explained through the fourth critical question of the well-known PLC at Work process: "How will we extend the learning for students who are already proficient?" (DuFour et al., 2016, p. 36).

   We would also like to clarify a few vocabulary items in the initial question. The first is regarding Gifted and Talented Education. It is our personal opinion that students should not be given labels. We see too often students being placed into groups by label (i.e., the "low" or "high" group, or "gifted"). When interventions and extensions are targeted, they are based on skills—either acquired or missing—and then the necessary supports are provided. We have seen students placed in groups identified as "low" in reading without targeting why they are low in reading. Simply grouping by ability won't achieve results. However, providing targeted supports for students who struggle with vowel blends and digraphs *will* lead to improvements. Similarly, we have seen "high-achieving" students given 30 more math problems to do because they have already mastered the content being taught. Those students should be able to create a project that will extend their learning and stretch them beyond the essential grade-level content.

   The next vocabulary item we would like to clarify is "enrichment." Enrichment provides access to students through special subjects or content areas, such as the arts, technology, or robotics. All students must have access to enrichment opportunities on a campus. We have also witnessed equity issues where music instruction is only offered during an English learner development block of time on a campus. This would prevent an English learner from ever having the opportunity to learn how to play a musical instrument.

   So to summarize in short, extension opportunities are built into the schedule and provided as needed. Labels, such as "gifted," are removed, and all students are provided opportunities for extension when they have mastered essential learning targets. Last, enrichment is something all students have access to regardless of whether they need additional support in core subjects.

9. **Where do transitional kindergarten and kindergarten fit in?**

   The same guidelines apply to both. There should be a lead teacher on the schoolwide MTSS team representing the needs of transitional kindergarten and kindergarten students for academic and social supports aligned with the schoolwide MTSS goals. Consider this question: Are there essential skills (academic and social) transitional kindergarten and kindergarten students are expected to master?

   The answer should be yes, and there needs to be a collective response in each tier of support for students who are not responding.

10. **Are there standardized ways to determine when a child moves to the next tier of intervention or support? Perhaps guidelines or ideas beyond the 80/15/5 rule?**

    An MTSS must require interventions that are systematic—meaning the school has built in structures that ensure every student in need of additional help will receive it. Buffum et al. (2018) state that a systematic response is composed of five steps:

    1. Identify students who need help.
    2. Determine the right intervention to meet the students' learning needs.
    3. Monitor each student's progress to determine if the intervention is working.
    4. Revise if the student is not responding to the intervention.
    5. Extend once the student has mastered essential curriculum.

    The first step is the most critical and must be a flawless identification process. For this, Buffum and colleagues suggest three identification strategies: (1) universal screening, (2) team common assessments, and (3) a staff-recommended process.

11. **Why are student voices left out of decision-making, for example, on needs-based audits for PBIS and MTSS?**

    Student voice should be a part of decision-making. If it is not, your school is missing a key demographic—the user's experience. When Apple want to improve a product, who do they seek input from? The user. In education, when we want to improve a product, we seek input primarily from the adults who have created that experience for the user (in our case, students). So if we want to see how the user in a school setting is experiencing that environment, it is essential that we not simply invite but also actively seek out that voice to improve that experience for our students. Student representation on the behavior team has always been encouraged in a PBIS school in Grades 5 and higher, while also providing ways of surveying students' voice in the lower grades. Student voice is also a critical component of culturally responsive teaching and a culturally responsive school. When students know that their teachers and administrators are listening to them, mutual trust and respect will thrive. Furthermore, when students believe that they are being heard and actually influencing decisions on a campus, school will become more relevant to their lives. The goal in restorative practices is to give educators the time to hear a student, understand the student, and then create an appropriate and equal response for that student. So, to put it simply, student voice is critical in all elements of the educational experience and plays a role in any behavior initiatives implemented within the MTSS framework, including and beyond just PBIS.

Note: In the MTSS Model, we encourage the inclusivity of all research-based initiatives and interventions, and it is not just limited to PBIS or SEL for behavior and a literacy focus for academics.

CHAPTER 3

MTSS SCHOOL CASE STUDY SCENARIOS

In order to understand where to begin, it is important that you understand some of the most common scenarios affecting implementation of MTSS nationwide. Take a few minutes with your leadership team or MTSS team to read the following scenarios and identify which one or elements of a few you identify with the most.

Scenario 1: MTSS in Everything Everything School

The current leadership team at Everything Everything School does not use stakeholder feedback or data when discussing next steps or actions to improve academic or behavior success for students. The goals of the school are unclear and continuously changing, and no current data are available to present the various levels of need to all stakeholders regarding next steps and the new initiatives being implemented in each tier at the school. In fact, there is a large disconnect between what the school leadership claims as an array of programs, initiatives, and interventions happening at the school and what the teachers/staff say is actually happening.

> **You have been given the directive to establish an MTSS framework at the Scenario 1 school. What are your first starting actions?**
>
> _____
>
> _____
>
> _____
>
> _____

Scenario 2: MTSS in a District-Led School

The current district leadership attended an enlightening MTSS conference where they learned about the benefits of implementing MTSS in their schools districtwide. When they returned from the conference, they announced to their school site administration that they would all be implementing MTSS in their schools. The district office team provided an MTSS overview based on the information they found on their state-level website regarding MTSS and worked on hiring additional staff to help with implementation. The school site leaders did not feel equipped to implement MTSS at their sites and as a result did not know how to roll it out adequately to their staff. In addition, each school received additional human resources support (i.e., additional days' service of a school psychologist, intervention specialist, counselor, and social worker). These additional resources were able to support each site with regard to MTSS; however, the extent of their support was dictated and monitored by the district office leadership, causing a disconnect between what each school site actually needed from this additional support staff and what they were actually doing at the sites.

You have been given the directive to establish an MTSS framework at the Scenario 2 school. What are your first starting actions?

Scenario 3: MTSS in a Site-Led School

A site leader decides with his site-level leadership team that it is time to implement MTSS in their school. Although the team members do not have formal training in MTSS implementation, they are eager and ready to learn and grow with the input of their staff and stakeholders. This school is known and recognized at the state level for model implementation of RTI and PLC, so they are not afraid of implementation of research-based support at the school. The staff and stakeholders are also eager to learn how MTSS differs from what they are currently doing at their site; they are open to its implementation but do not know where to begin. In addition, the district office leadership does not have a clear understanding of MTSS implementation and lacks the ability to efficiently support these efforts.

You have been given the directive to establish an MTSS framework at the Scenario 3 school. What are your first starting actions?

Now that you have had an opportunity to process through some of these common MTSS implementation scenarios, take a few minutes with your leadership team to write down your school's current state of MTSS implementation.

Write your current MTSS scenario here.

What is it that you need in order to know where to start based on your current scenario state?

Now that you have read and begun to process some of the common MTSS implementation scenarios, including in your own school, it is time to assess your current readiness and MTSS implementation anxiety level.

What questions do you have at this point of the book?

What is your implementation anxiety level from 1 (*not at all anxious*) to 5 (*very anxious*)? If you scored yourself a 3 or higher, take a deep breath and remember—you are going to tackle this with your team, one MTSS start-up indicator at a time.

PART III

WHERE DO WE START?

CHAPTER 4

ASSESSING YOUR MTSS READINESS AND CURRENT STATE

Dedicate some intentional time with your leadership team to complete the MTSS Readiness Screener and MTSS start-up guide audit. This information will help you and your team identify your areas of need so that as you begin to delve into the next chapter—where the 10 MTSS start-up guide indicators are defined with practical tools for implementation—you will be able to fill in your identified areas of need in each tier of implementation. It is important to understand where your school lands on the readiness scale and the MTSS start-up guide audit to avoid setting yourself up for implementation failure even before you begin. This screener and audit should not be used as the sole evaluation of MTSS readiness or an indictment of your current state but, rather, as a reliable starting point. Starting the MTSS work is complex because there are a lot of moving parts and multiple initiatives, so it is important to use the next chapter in this book to help clear away some of the implementation fog and begin identifying how all members of the school team will work together to move "the ship" in the same direction toward equity, access, and inclusivity for the students we serve. The MTSS start-up guide indicators, defined in the next chapter, will help you begin filling in the areas of your MTSS implementation that are a priority. When you are able to show evidence of each of these indicators, your school team will then begin to develop and continue improving your effective implementation. *Note:* Do not get overwhelmed trying to implement all 10 indicators at once. Take one indicator at a time, process through it with your team, and then move on to the next one.

What Is the MTSS Readiness Screener?

The MTSS Readiness Screener is designed to help your leadership team take an honest look at what needs to be in place prior to beginning implementation. It is recommended that a school leader, along with his or her leadership team, complete the MTSS Readiness Screener. The goal is to have a score of 15 points or higher out of 18 points total to indicate adequate readiness.

Note: If you have already begun implementation, take the screener to ensure that a solid foundation is in place to do the work well.

Who Should Complete the MTSS Readiness Screener?

In an effort to obtain accurate baseline readiness information, the MTSS team, with representation of the school's system in each tier (i.e., school psychologist, counselor, specialists, etc.), should complete the screener. If you do not have an MTSS team established at the time of this baseline screener, the administrator of the school should complete it in collaboration with his or her leadership team.

MTSS READINESS SCREENER					
Readiness factor	0: Not ready	1: In progress	2: Ready for implementation	Readiness factor score	Next step action/date
Vision/mission aligned	Vision and mission are not aligned to MTSS work.	Vision and mission work alignment has begun but is not completed.	Vision and mission are aligned and include stakeholder input.		
Need	The need is not made clear to the stakeholders.	The need is clear to some but not to others.	The need is made clear and supported by data.		
Willingness	The leadership and staff have not made implementation a priority.	There is 50% willingness to implement among the stakeholders.	The leadership and staff are willing to implement.		
Funding available	Funding is not available or restructured to meet the needs of implementation.	Funding is being reevaluated, but no adjustments have been made at this time.	Funding is allocated and prioritized for implementation needs.		
Accountability structure in place	Implementation is optional, with no clear outcomes identified.	There are some components of accountability in place but not others.	Goals are set, and monthly accountability checks for all stakeholders in the system are in place.		
Leadership capacity	The leadership does not have a clear understanding of MTSS implementation.	The leadership is beginning to take steps to build capacity in MTSS implementation.	The leadership is committed to building staff capacity on an ongoing basis.		
Ability to implement and monitor progress	The leadership does not have the training or tools to implement.	The leadership is beginning to understand MTSS implementation, but they still do not feel as if they are ready to fully lead implementation.	The leadership has the ability to lead the school in implementation and monitoring of key MTSS actions.		

(Continued)

(Continued)

Readiness factor	0: Not ready	1: In progress	2: Ready for implementation	Readiness factor score	Next step action/date
Time commitment	Individual programs or initiatives have consumed the time of the leadership.	Time has been allotted but is not consistently utilized for MTSS implementation.	The leadership has allotted and will continue to allow adequate time for MTSS implementation.		
Readiness factor score: ____/18 points					
15 points and above = Ready to begin the work					
12–14 points = In progress to begin the work					
13 points and below = Need improvement to begin the work					

 Available for download at resources.corwin.com/MTSSStartupGuide.

What Is the MTSS Start-Up Assessment?

The MTSS Start-Up Assessment is designed to assess the 10 starting indicators in MTSS start-up implementation. It is a tool designed to help with gauging a baseline on MTSS implementation and can also be used for ongoing progress monitoring of the foundation in schools. The indicator evidencing a strong MTSS foundation on the MTSS Start-up Assessment is an overall score of 80% or higher, which is equivalent to 16 points or more out of 20 points. You will use the results of this assessment to conduct a gap analysis and gain an understanding of where your system is in relation to the 10 essential indicators. It is important that honest responses are provided for all the items in this assessment because the information gained from this assessment data is used to guide your next-step actions.

Who Should Complete the MTSS Start-Up Assessment?

In an effort to obtain accurate baseline information, the MTSS team, with representation of the school's system in each tier (i.e., school psychologist, counselor, specialists, etc.), should complete the assessment. If you do not have an MTSS team established at the time of this baseline assessment, the administrator of the school should complete it in collaboration with his or her leadership team.

MTSS START-UP ASSESSMENT			
Indicator	0: Not in place	1: In progress	2: In place with success criteria evidence
Indicator 1: Establish an MTSS team (i.e., team-driven and shared leadership). Indicator score: ___	There is no established MTSS team.	There is an established MTSS team, but there is limited representation on the team. Meetings are inconsistently held and data are not utilized.	MTSS team is established (representation from each tier in academics and behavior). MTSS team meets at least monthly. MTSS team utilizes a variety of data points and has an agenda (for each tier) during meetings. Administrator leads the MTSS team.

Indicator	0: Not in place	1: In progress	2: In place with success criteria evidence
Indicator 2: Assess stakeholder beliefs, perceptions, shared values, and identity, and establish the mission and purpose of the MTSS team and all stakeholders (i.e., families, school, community, partnerships, etc.). Indicator score: ___	Stakeholder beliefs and perceptions are not assessed.	Some stakeholder beliefs and perceptions are assessed, but key stakeholders remain left out. Information gathered from stakeholders has not yet been utilized to establish the mission and purpose of the MTSS team.	MTSS team develops its mission and vision based on stakeholder feedback. MTSS team establishes the mission and purpose of MTSS in the school. MTSS team has methods of collecting ongoing feedback from stakeholders, which include at least families, school staff, community, and partnerships. MTSS team has established collective commitments for MTSS implementation. Evidence of student voice.
Indicator 3: Establish and apportion roles and responsibilities among MTSS team members and all stakeholders (i.e., shared ownership and responsibility). Indicator score: ___	Roles and responsibilities are not established.	MTSS team roles and responsibilities are beginning to develop, but there is limited shared ownership and responsibility.	MTSS team's roles and responsibilities are clear. All stakeholders understand their roles and responsibilities toward the schoolwide MTSS goals. There is an accountability process in place for shared ownership and responsibility toward the MTSS goals. There are ongoing (at least quarterly) check-ins on all MTSS team members and all MTSS schoolwide stakeholders on their roles and responsibilities. MTSS roles and responsibilities audit is complete, and all gaps are filled in.
Indicator 4: Audit current organizational structures and evidence-based practices (i.e., tiered processes/continuum of supports in place, programs, teams, human resources/expertise/ training, initiatives, interventions) for academics and behavior. Indicator score: ___	There has been no current audit conducted of organizational structures and evidence-based practices for academics or behavior.	The MTSS team are in the early stages of auditing their academic and behavior organizational structures and evidence-based practices. Entrance or exit points are not consistently established for each tier of support.	MTSS Audit: Menu of Responses, Initiatives, Interventions, Programs is completed, and all gaps are filled in. All stakeholders understand what evidence-based interventions and responses are available in each tier. There are clear entrance and exit points for each of the tiers of support for both academics and behavior. There is a process for developing new interventions and supports based on MTSS student need data points.
Indicator 5: Assess the current state of academic and behavior instruction based on multiple data points (i.e., data-based problem-solving and decision-making). Indicator score: ___	There is no assessment of the current state of academic and behavior instruction based on data.	The MTSS team are in the early stages of assessing the current academic and behavior instruction but do not have multiple data points to help them make decisions.	Needed data are identified for both academics and behavior in each tier. Both quantitative and qualitative data are utilized. Data are updated and available for MTSS meetings. Processes are set to ensure accountability of current data. All students are represented in the data utilized.

(Continued)

(Continued)

Indicator	0: Not in place	1: In progress	2: In place with success criteria evidence
Indicator 6: Develop and share MTSS SMART goals and actions for academics and behavior (i.e., based on assessment, screener, trend, qualitative, and quantitative data). Indicator score: ___	MTSS SMART goals have not been developed.	MTSS team has begun the development of MTSS SMART goals based on stakeholder input. Actions are not developed based on academic and behavior SMART goals.	MTSS team creates schoolwide goals (i.e., at least one schoolwide academic goal and one schoolwide behavior goal). All stakeholders contribute to goal development. Progress-monitoring structures are in place for every goal. Short-term and long-term goal attainments are celebrated and shared with all stakeholders. Process for relevant and timely feedback needs to be communicated for a team's progress toward its goals. Completed the MTSS Planning Guide.
Indicator 7: Set up a progress-monitoring system/benchmarks for MTSS, and ensure that assessment and data are up-to-date and available for decision-making. Indicator score: ___	There is no progress-monitoring system/benchmarks set up for MTSS.	Progress-monitoring system/benchmarks are being developed to help with decision-making. MTSS Team Agenda is not completed consistently (i.e., problem statement and next-step action sections based on each tier are inconsistently completed or discussed).	MTSS Team Agenda is completed at least monthly. Problem statement and next-step actions based on tiers are articulated in documents. Evidence of implementation of the actions for each tier. Share-out process with key stakeholders.
Indicator 8: Set up clear communication structures between the MTSS team and all stakeholders. Indicator score: ___	There are no clear communication structures set up.	MTSS team is in the process of developing clear communication structures between the team and all stakeholders.	Designee from the MTSS team is the lead on communication from the meetings (at least monthly). Staff meetings have an embedded MTSS time for communication and sharing opportunities. MTSS agendas are transparent and accessible. Stakeholders have an opportunity to contribute to MTSS agenda items. There are safe structures in place for all stakeholders to provide information to the MTSS team at all times.

Indicator	0: Not in place	1: In progress	2: In place with success criteria evidence
Indicator 9: Set up ongoing MTSS professional learning for all stakeholders. Indicator score: ___	There is no ongoing MTSS professional learning for all stakeholders.	The MTSS team is in the initial stages of developing professional learning opportunities for all stakeholders. Limited funding is available for ongoing professional learning for all stakeholders, but the team is working diligently to provide opportunities.	The MTSS professional learning calendar is set and available to all stakeholders (includes quarterly training opportunities for all stakeholder groups), with room for adjustments as needed based on stakeholder needs. There is internal capacity building within the MTSS team to provide ongoing professional learning and support. Multiple modalities of professional learning are provided (in person or online). Funding is allocated toward professional opportunities for all stakeholders.
Indicator 10: Set up a process for ongoing evaluation and continuous improvement of MTSS implementation effectiveness and fidelity. Indicator score: ___	There is no process in place for ongoing evaluation and continuous improvement of MTSS implementation.	MTSS team has identified an accountability structure but utilizes it inconsistently. There are no consistent fidelity checks in place.	There is an accountability structure in place for MTSS implementation (norms, collective agreements). All MTSS members understand and agree on the evaluation and continuous-improvement process. Implementation fidelity checks are in place at least quarterly.

Total score: _____/20 points

Goal is 80% or higher

Based on the MTSS start-up guide screener and assessment you completed, identify areas of need below:

GAP IDENTIFIED	PROBLEM STATEMENT (CONVERT THE IDENTIFIED GAP INTO A PROBLEM STATEMENT)	DESIRED FUTURE STATE

CHAPTER 5

MTSS START-UP GUIDE
A Blueprint for Start-Up Implementation

To build a strong implementation of MTSS in your school, 10 essential indicators must be in place. This chapter presents each of the 10 starting indicators of the MTSS Model implementation.

The 10 Indicators of MTSS Implementation		
1		**Indicator 1:** Establish an MTSS team (i.e., team-driven and shared leadership).
2		**Indicator 2:** Assess stakeholder beliefs, perceptions, shared values, and identity, and establish the mission and purpose of the MTSS team and all stakeholders (i.e., families, school, community, partnerships, etc.).
3		**Indicator 3:** Establish and apportion roles and responsibilities among MTSS team members and all stakeholders (i.e., shared ownership and responsibility).
4		**Indicator 4:** Audit current organizational structures and evidence-based practices (i.e., tiered processes/continuum of supports in place, programs, teams, human resources/expertise/training, initiatives, interventions) for academics and behavior.
5		**Indicator 5:** Assess the current state of academic and behavior instruction based on multiple data points (i.e., data-based problem-solving and decision-making).
6		**Indicator 6:** Develop and share MTSS SMART* goals and actions for academics and behavior (i.e., based on assessment, screener, trend, qualitative, and quantitative data).
7		**Indicator 7:** Set up a progress-monitoring system/benchmarks for MTSS, and ensure that assessment and data are up-to-date and available for decision-making.

Icon Source: istock.com/appleuzr

*Note: SMART refers to specific, measurable, achievable, realistic, and timely.

(Continued)

(Continued)

8		**Indicator 8:** Set up clear communication structures between the MTSS team and all stakeholders.
9		**Indicator 9:** Set up ongoing MTSS professional learning for all stakeholders.
10		**Indicator 10:** Set up a process for ongoing evaluation and continuous improvement of MTSS implementation effectiveness and fidelity.

Icon Source: istock.com/appleuzr

The following aids are provided for each of the 10 indicators:

☐ Description of the indicator and success criteria

☐ Practical tools and implementation processes from the field

☐ Red flags and tips to consider

☐ Commitment for indicator implementation

How Best to Utilize This Section of the Chapter

As you read this section, process all the components of the indicators one at a time. Consider how you are going to proceed through these indicators and utilize the processes and tools provided. Also, make a time-bound commitment after starting each indicator to ensure that progress is being made. Remember, all this will not happen in one day; it is better to build a strong foundation than rush headlong into implementation. The suggested timeline for completion/mastery of these 10 indicators is 1–2 years.

Establish an MTSS team
(i.e., team-driven and shared leadership)

INDICATOR
#1

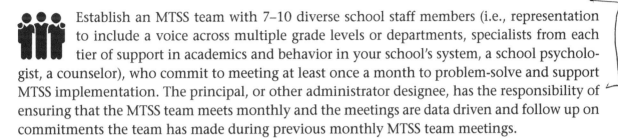 Establish an MTSS team with 7–10 diverse school staff members (i.e., representation to include a voice across multiple grade levels or departments, specialists from each tier of support in academics and behavior in your school's system, a school psychologist, a counselor), who commit to meeting at least once a month to problem-solve and support MTSS implementation. The principal, or other administrator designee, has the responsibility of ensuring that the MTSS team meets monthly and the meetings are data driven and follow up on commitments the team has made during previous monthly MTSS team meetings.

Success criteria

▶ MTSS team is established (representation from each tier in academics and behavior)

▶ MTSS team meets at least monthly

▶ MTSS team utilizes a variety of data points and has an agenda (from each tier) during meetings

▶ Administrator leads the MTSS team

Practical tool from the field and implementation process: MTSS Team Organization Prompt

Process for this tool

Step 1: With your leadership team, complete the organization prompt.

Step 2: Identify areas of need.

Step 3: Communicate this completed prompt with all stakeholders for feedback.

Icon Source: istock.com/appleuzr

SAMPLE MTSS ORGANIZATION PROMPT

WHO IS ON THE TEAM?

Principal, vice principal, psychologist, lead teachers, SPED teacher, teacher on special assignment, and other stakeholder representative(s)

WHAT IS THE PURPOSE OF THE TEAM?

Implementation is a process that turns strategies and plans into actions in order to accomplish strategic objectives and goals—an evidence-based model of schooling that uses data-based problem-solving to integrate academic and behavior instruction and intervention.

HOW OFTEN DOES THE TEAM MEET?

Once a month at a minimum

WHAT DATA ARE UTILIZED?

Academic data, staff input, behavioral data, SEL, student input, attendance, SMART goals progress-monitoring data from each tier, and other stakeholder input (e.g., school process data; subgroup/demographic data; achievement data; discipline data by location, incident, time of day, referring staff, and referred student; and perception data—such as empathy interviews*—from students, staff, and parents)

HOW ARE INFORMATION AND INPUT GATHERED FROM OTHER TEACHER STAKEHOLDERS NOT ON THE TEAM?

Through the MTSS leads (roles and responsibilities)

DO YOU HAVE SUBTEAMS OF THE LARGER MTSS TEAM WITH A FOCUS ON SPECIFIC TIERS OR BEHAVIOR?

Yes, three teams: (1) prevention (meet monthly), (2) intervention (meet biweekly), and (3) remediation (meet weekly)

*A template for empathy interviews is available for download at resources.corwin.com/MTSSStartupGuide

MTSS TEAM ORGANIZATION PROMPT TEMPLATE

WHO IS ON THE TEAM?

_____

_____

WHAT IS THE PURPOSE OF THE TEAM?

_____

_____

_____

_____

HOW OFTEN DOES THE TEAM MEET?

_____

_____

WHAT DATA ARE UTILIZED?

_____

_____

_____

_____

_____

_____

HOW ARE INFORMATION AND INPUT GATHERED FROM OTHER TEACHER STAKEHOLDERS NOT ON THE TEAM?

_____

_____

DO YOU HAVE SUBTEAMS OF THE LARGER MTSS TEAM WITH A FOCUS ON SPECIFIC TIERS OR BEHAVIOR?

_____

_____

Red flags and tips to consider

RED FLAG	TIP TO CONSIDER
Principal or administrator is not involved in MTSS implementation.	Principal or administrator needs to have the capacity to lead the charge.
MTSS implementation has not been established to be a priority.	MTSS needs to be set as a top priority at the school.
MTSS meetings are often cancelled.	MTSS meetings should never be cancelled and should be scheduled months in advance, if not calendared for the year.
Data are not utilized in decision-making.	Make it an expectation to have updated data at all MTSS meetings (e.g., school process data; subgroup/demographic data; achievement data; discipline data by location, incident, time of day, referring staff, and referred student; and perception data from students, staff, and parents).
There is no adequate staff representation from each tier in MTSS implementation for both academics and behavior at the school.	Make sure there is representation from all tiers of support in the school system (e.g., SPED, reading intervention, English language development, the school psychologist, counselors).

INDICATOR 1

Commitment for Implementation

Establish an MTSS team (i.e., team-driven and shared leadership)		
COMMITMENT	SUCCESS CRITERIA (EVIDENCE OF IMPLEMENTATION)	BY WHOM/WHEN

Assess stakeholder beliefs, perceptions, shared values, and identity, and establish the mission and purpose of the MTSS team and all stakeholders
(i.e., families, school, community, partnerships, etc.)

The MTSS team intentionally assesses stakeholder beliefs, perceptions, shared values, and identity on the school campus. Based on all stakeholder information, the mission and vision are established, and everyone involved understands the purpose of establishing equity, access, and inclusivity for every child. There are processes and structures in place to allow for ongoing stakeholder feedback and shared leadership opportunities, which includes but is not limited to families, school staff, community, and partnerships. The MTSS team provides student voice opportunities when implementing MTSS.

Success criteria

MTSS team develops its mission and vision based on stakeholder feedback

- ‣ MTSS team establishes the purpose and identity of MTSS in the school
- ‣ MTSS team has methods of collecting ongoing stakeholder feedback, which includes at least families, school staff, community, and partnerships
- ‣ MTSS team has established collective commitments for MTSS implementation
- ‣ Evidence of student voice

Practical tools from the field and implementation process: School Collective Commitments Form, Schoolwide Roadmap Visual of Collective Commitments, and Stakeholder Identification and Action-Planning Form

Process for these tools

Step 1: Review the mission and vision statement.

Step 2: Individually brainstorm attitudes, beliefs, and behaviors that must be in place to accomplish the mission and vision. This step answers the question "How must we behave to accomplish our school's fundamental purpose (mission) and compelling future (vision)?"

Step 3: In teams, share and identify the attitudes, beliefs, and behaviors necessary to accomplish the mission and vision statement.

Step 4: Draft no more than five statements of these commitments using "We will . . . "

Step 5: Discuss as a team, address any challenges, and revise draft statements as necessary.

Step 6: All teams share their statements or can engage in a gallery walk.

Step 7: Combine common statements and the majority vote process using sticky dots or Post-it Notes.

SAMPLE SCHOOL COLLECTIVE COMMITMENTS FORM

School name: *The Foundation of Ronald W. Reagan Elementary*

Our mission: *To increase student achievement for all students*

Our vision: *We envision that our school will take responsibility for the achievement of all students' academic and social well-being by working as a community to provide an engaging academic environment focused on student learning.*

Our collective commitments:

To fulfill our fundamental purpose and become the school we describe in our vision statement, each member of the staff commits to the following:

- *We will view all students as our own to ensure equity, inclusivity, and access in order to maximize each student's academic and social well-being.*
- *We will teach the essential learnings of our agreed-on curriculum.*
- *We will monitor each student's learning on an ongoing basis through classroom and team-developed formative assessments.*
- *We will use evidence of student learning and social well-being to inform and improve our practice and to better meet the needs of individual students.*
- *We will work with our collaborative team to achieve our SMART goals.*
- *We will utilize the most effective instructional practices to foster student learning.*
- *We will frequently keep parents informed of their child's progress.*

As a result of that commitment:

- *The staff continuously seeks ways to improve their practices to support student learning and social well-being.*
- *The school is characterized by a collaborative culture and the use of student data to inform improvement decisions.*
- *The learning and social well-being of each student is monitored on an ongoing basis.*

Our schoolwide goals:

We will monitor the following indicators to mark our progress:

1. *Reduce the rate of students not achieving on grade level.*
2. *Increase the percentage of students successful in the most rigorous curriculum in each subject and grade level.*
3. *Increase student achievement on local and state high-stakes assessments.*
4. *Reduce the rate of students not meeting schoolwide and classroom behavior goals (i.e., suspensions, referrals, detention, etc).*

SCHOOL COLLECTIVE COMMITMENTS FORM TEMPLATE

School name: _____

Our mission:

_____

_____

Our vision:

_____

_____

_____

Our collective commitments:

To fulfill our fundamental purpose and become the school we describe in our vision statement, each member of the staff commits to the following:

▸ We will_____

_____

▸ We will_____

_____

▸ We will_____

_____

▸ We will_____

_____

▸ We will_____

_____

▸ We will_____

_____

▸ We will_____

_____

As a result of that commitment:

▶ _____
_____

▶ _____
_____

▶ _____
_____

▶ _____
_____

▶ _____
_____

Our schoolwide goals:

We will monitor the following indicators to mark our progress:

1. _____
_____

2. _____
_____

3. _____
_____

4. _____
_____

5. _____
_____

6. _____
_____

Schoolwide roadmap visual of the Collective Commitments sample

Mission	To increase student achievement for *all* students		
Vision	We envision that our school will take responsibility for the achievement of *all* students' academic and personal growth by working as a community to provide an engaging academic environment focused on student learning.		
Goals	Increase *all* students' achievement	Close the achievement gap	Ensure a safe environment
Strategies	PLC and RTI MTSS UDL Family and community partnerships Student voice		
Values	Collaborative, equitable, and inclusive culture		
Beliefs	All students can and will learn	"All" means *all*	Don't blame the kids

Schoolwide roadmap visual of the Collective Commitments template

Mission			
Vision			
Goals			
Strategies			
Values			
Beliefs			

Stakeholder Identification and Action-Planning Form

List of some common stakeholders as a reference:

☐ Board members

☐ Parents and community

☐ Union association/leadership

☐ Certificated staff

☐ Classified staff

☐ LCAP writer or team

☐ District leadership

☐ Students

☐ District-level parent groups

☐ School staff

SMART Goal 1

Write your MTSS SMART Goal 1 statement here:

Action Description	Person(S) Responsible	Stakeholder Impact (Which Stakeholder Might This Action Affect?)	Stakeholder Input Strategy (What Method Was Used For Collecting Stakeholder Input?)	Date To Begin	Date Due	Resources Needed	Outcome
Sample: Educate school board on PBIS initiative	Principal	School board, community	School board: individual phone interviews Community: online survey to parents	August 2 board meeting	August 2	PPT overview for the school board, one-page overview community handouts	School board has a clear understanding of the why around this initiative and the goal for students

Action Description	Person(S) Responsible	Stakeholder Impact (Which Stakeholder Might This Action Affect?)	Stakeholder Input Strategy (What Method Was Used For Collecting Stakeholder Input?)	Date To Begin	Date Due	Resources Needed	Outcome

Note: LCAP, Local Control and Accountability Plan.

Red flags and tips to consider

RED FLAG	TIP TO CONSIDER
Shared leadership is not practiced; decisions are made and executed solely by the principal.	Have a process set up for shared leadership opportunities. Develop collective commitments on these agreements ahead of time.
MTSS team members and stakeholders do not know the purpose of MTSS.	Frequently educate members and stakeholders on their purpose on the MTSS team and the critical role they play in successful MTSS implementation.
No one knows the mission and vision of the school and how it is aligned to MTSS implementation.	Revisit the mission and vision together, and make sure they are adjusted to meet the needs of MTSS implementation. Educate all stakeholders on the mission and vision and how they align to MTSS.
Parents, community, and partnerships do not feel as if they can contribute in any way.	Develop ongoing opportunities for parent, community, and partnership involvement. Think out of the box, and help make them feel a part of the school family.
Student voice is not considered.	Include a student representative or representatives to rotate providing input to the MTSS team about their needs for success.

INDICATOR 2

Commitment for Implementation

Assess stakeholder beliefs, perceptions, shared values, and identity, and establish the mission and purpose of the MTSS team and all stakeholders (i.e., families, school, community, partnerships, etc.)		
COMMITMENT	SUCCESS CRITERIA (EVIDENCE OF IMPLEMENTATION)	BY WHOM/WHEN

 Available for download at resources.corwin.com/MTSSStartupGuide

INDICATOR #3

Establish and apportion roles and responsibilities among MTSS team members and all stakeholders
(i.e., shared ownership and responsibility)

The MTSS team works with all stakeholders to ensure that everyone is clear on their roles and responsibilities as part of the MTSS team and/or as a contributing stakeholder toward the entire schoolwide MTSS model in each tier of support. There is an understanding of shared ownership and responsibility toward the schoolwide MTSS goals.

Success criteria

▶ MTSS team's roles and responsibilities are clear

▶ All stakeholders understand their roles and responsibilities toward the schoolwide MTSS goals

▶ There is an accountability process in place for shared ownership and responsibility toward the MTSS goals

▶ There are ongoing (at least quarterly) check-ins on all MTSS team members and all MTSS schoolwide stakeholders on their roles and responsibilities

▶ MTSS roles and responsibilities audit is complete, and all gaps are filled in

Practical tool from the field and implementation process: MTSS Pyramid Audit: Roles and Responsibilities and MTSS Pyramid Audit: Roles and Responsibilities—Expanded Form

Process for this tool

Step 1: List all the different team meetings that are held at your campus.

Step 2: Give the purpose of each item listed.

Step 3: Draw a star next to any that require using data to make decisions for academic or behavior supports.

Step 4: Complete the MTSS Pyramid Audit and the Expanded Form by answering the prompts for each tier.

MTSS Audit: Roles and Responsibilities

BEHAVIOR/SEL

MTSS

Who is on the team? Who is the lead? Do you have representation from all tiers of support? How often do you meet? Is it at least once a month? What are the MTSS team SMART goals? How do you know if what you are doing is working or not? What data are utilized? Where are the problem statements and success criteria established?

Tier 3
Few
REMEDIATION

Who is accountable for this tier? Who is the lead? Who are the behavior specialists? Are they trained? How often do they meet? Is it at least weekly? What are the SMART goals aligned with MTSS? What are the structures or supports for supporting multiyear behavior/SEL gaps (remediation)? How are they communicated, and how is progress shared with MTSS team? How do students access Tier 3 (i.e., in and out)? How do you know if Tier 3 (general or SPED) is working? What data are utilized? Where are the problem statements and success criteria established? How do stakeholders (i.e., teachers) access ongoing support of Tier 3?

Tier 2
Some
INTERVENTION

Who is accountable for this tier? Who is the lead? How often do they meet? Is it at least twice a month? What are the SMART goals aligned with MTSS? What are the structures or supports for reteaching opportunities (intervention)? How are they communicated, and how is progress shared with MTSS team? How do students access Tier 2 (in and out)? How do you know if Tier 2 is working? What data are utilized? Where are the problem statements and success criteria established? How to stakeholders (i.e., teachers) access support of Tier 2?

Tier 1
All
PREVENTION

Who is accountable for this tier? Who is the lead? What are the nonnegotiables in every classroom and school wide (prevention)? How do you observe and measure? How often do they meet? Is it at least once a month? What are the SMART goals aligned with MTSS (i.e., every student one level up) for this tier? How do you know if what you are doing is working or not? What data are utilized? Where are the problem statements and success criteria established? How are they communicated, and how is progress shared with MTSS team? What does universal screening look like? How do students access Tier 1?

ACADEMICS

Who is accountable for this tier? Who is the lead? Who are the specialists? Are they trained? How often do they meet? Is it at least weekly? What are the SMART goals aligned with MTSS? What are the structures or supports for supporting multiyear academic gaps (remediation)? How are they communicated, and how is progress shared with MTSS team? How do students access Tier 3 (i.e., in and out)? How do you know if Tier 3 (general or SPED) is working? What data are utilized? Where are the problem statements and success criteria established? How do stakeholders (i.e., teachers) access ongoing support of Tier 3?

Who is accountable for this tier? Who is the lead? How often do they meet? Is it at least twice a month? What are the SMART goals aligned with MTSS? What are the structures or supports for reteaching opportunities (intervention)? How are they communicated, and how is progress shared with MTSS team? How do students access Tier 2 (in and out)? How do you know if Tier 2 is working? What data are utilized? Where are the problem statements and success criteria established? How do stakeholders (i.e., teachers) access support of Tier 2?

Who is accountable for this tier? Who is the lead? What are the nonnegotiables in every classroom (prevention)? How do you observe and measure? How often do they meet? Is it at least once a month? What are the SMART goals aligned with MTSS (i.e., every student one level up) for this tier? How do you know if what you are doing is working or not? What data are utilized? Where are the problem statements and success criteria established? How are they communicated, and how is progress shared with MTSS team? What does universal screening look like? How do students access Tier 1?

MTSS Audit: Roles and Responsibilities–Expanded Form

MTSS TEAM	
QUESTION PROMPT	**RESPONSE/EVIDENCE**
Who is on the team?	
Who is the lead?	
Do they have representation from all tiers of support?	
How often do they meet? Is it at least once a month?	
What are the MTSS team SMART goals?	
How will you know that what you are doing is working?	
What data are utilized?	
Where are the problem statements and success criteria established?	

TIER 1 ACADEMICS	
QUESTION PROMPT	RESPONSE/EVIDENCE
Who is accountable for this tier?	
Who is the lead?	
What are the nonnegotiables in every classroom (prevention)?	
How do they observe and measure?	
How often do they meet? Is it at least once a month?	
What are the SMART goals aligned with MTSS (i.e., every student one level up) for this tier?	
How will you know that what you are doing is working?	
What data are utilized?	
Where are the problem statements and success criteria established?	
How are they communicated, and how is progress shared with the MTSS team?	
What does universal screening look like?	
How do students access Tier 2?	

(Continued)

(Continued)

TIER 1 BEHAVIOR/SEL	
QUESTION PROMPT	RESPONSE/EVIDENCE
Who is accountable for this tier?	
Who is the lead?	
What are the nonnegotiables in every classroom and schoolwide (prevention)?	
How do they observe and measure?	
How often do they meet? Is it at least once a month?	
What are the SMART goals aligned with MTSS (i.e., every student one level up) for this tier?	
How will you know that what you are doing is working?	
What data are utilized?	
Where are the problem statements and success criteria established?	
How are they communicated, and how is progress shared with the MTSS team?	
What does universal screening look like?	
How do students access Tier 2?	

TIER 2 ACADEMICS	
QUESTION PROMPT	RESPONSE/EVIDENCE
Who is accountable for this tier?	
Who is the lead?	
How often do they meet? Is it at least twice a month?	
What are the SMART goals aligned with MTSS?	
What are the structures or supports for reteaching opportunities (intervention)?	
How are they communicated, and how is progress shared with the MTSS team? How do students access Tier 2 (entrance and exit criteria)?	
How do you know if Tier 2 is working?	
What data are utilized?	
Where are the problem statements and success criteria established?	
How do students access Tier 3? How to stakeholders (i.e., teachers) access support of Tier 3?	

(Continued)

(Continued)

TIER 2 BEHAVIOR/SEL	
QUESTION PROMPT	RESPONSE/EVIDENCE
Who is accountable for this tier?	
Who is the lead?	
How often do they meet? Is it at least twice a month?	
What are the SMART goals aligned with MTSS?	
What are the structures or supports for reteaching opportunities (intervention)?	
How are they communicated, and how is progress shared with the MTSS team?	
How do students access Tier 2 (entrance and exit criteria)?	
How do you know if Tier 2 is working?	
What data are utilized?	
Where are the problem statements and success criteria established?	
How do students access Tier 3? How do stakeholders (i.e., teachers) access support of Tier 3?	

TIER 3 ACADEMICS	
QUESTION PROMPT	RESPONSE/EVIDENCE
Who is accountable for this tier?	
Who is the lead?	
Who are the specialists? Are they trained?	
How often do they meet? Is it at least weekly?	
What are the SMART goals aligned with MTSS?	
What are the structures or supports for supporting multiyear academic gaps (remediation)?	
How are they communicated, and how is progress shared with the MTSS team?	
How do students access Tier 3 (entrance and exit criteria)?	
How do you know if Tier 3 (general education or SPED) is working?	
What data are utilized?	
Where are the problem statements and success criteria established?	
How do stakeholders (i.e., teachers) access ongoing support of Tier 3?	

(Continued)

(Continued)

TIER 3 BEHAVIOR/SEL	
QUESTION PROMPT	**RESPONSE/EVIDENCE**
Who is accountable for this tier?	
Who is the lead?	
Who are the behavior specialists? Are they trained?	
How often do they meet? Is it at least weekly?	
What are the SMART goals aligned with MTSS?	
What are the structures or supports for supporting multiyear behavior/SEL gaps (remediation)?	
How are they communicated, and is progress shared with the MTSS team?	
How do students access Tier 3 (entrance and exit criteria)?	
How do you know if Tier 3 (general or SPED) is working?	
What data are utilized?	
Where are the problem statements and success criteria established?	
How do stakeholders (i.e., teachers) access ongoing support of Tier 3?	

MTSS Audit: Roles and Responsibilities template

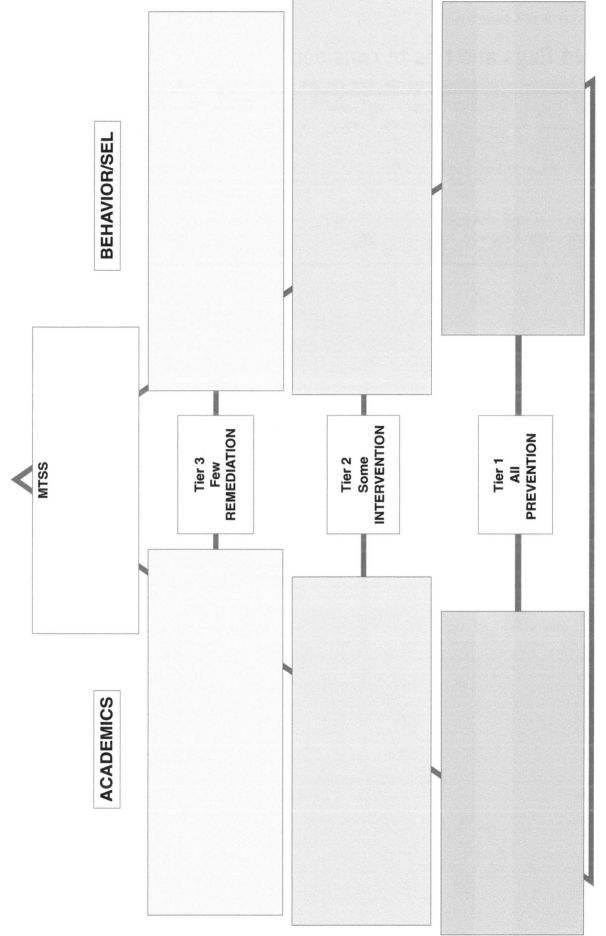

MTSS

BEHAVIOR/SEL

ACADEMICS

Tier 3
Few
REMEDIATION

Tier 2
Some
INTERVENTION

Tier 1
All
PREVENTION

Available for download at resources.corwin.com/MTSSStartupGuide

Red flags and tips to consider

RED FLAG	TIP TO CONSIDER
Principal is making all implementation decisions without consulting the MTSS team and relevant stakeholders.	Be transparent with the MTSS team and stakeholders about data and decision-making.
Roles and responsibilities of all are not clear.	Set up a document that identifies everyone's roles and responsibilities in each tier. Make sure all stakeholders understand what tiers they are supporting.
Poor communication and understanding of one another's roles and responsibilities.	Provide opportunities for all stakeholders to understand one another's roles and responsibilities toward schoolwide MTSS goals.

INDICATOR 3

Commitment for Implementation

Establish and apportion roles and responsibilities among MTSS team members and all stakeholders (i.e., shared ownership and responsibility)		
COMMITMENT	SUCCESS CRITERIA (EVIDENCE OF IMPLEMENTATION)	BY WHOM/WHEN

Audit current organizational structures and evidence-based practices

(i.e., tiered processes/continuum of supports in place, programs, teams, human resources/expertise/training, initiatives, interventions) for academics and behavior

Audit current organizational structures and evidence-based practices for academics and behavior in each tier offered at the school. Identify and place evidence-based interventions and supports for each tier for academics and behavior. Include processes for accessing each tier of support and progress monitoring of implementation. Educate all stakeholders on tiered supports available at the school.

Success criteria

▶ MTSS Audit: Menu of Responses, Initiatives, Interventions, Programs is completed, and all gaps are filled in

▶ All stakeholders understand what evidence-based interventions and responses are available in each tier

▶ There are clear entrance and exit points for each of the tiers of support for both academics and behavior

▶ There is a process for developing new interventions and supports based on MTSS student need data points

Practical tool from the field and implementation process: MTSS Audit: Menu of Responses, Initiatives, Interventions, Programs

Process for this tool

Step 1: Provide a template of this audit or organizational graphic to all stakeholders.

Step 2: Have stakeholders list all the responses, initiatives, interventions, and programs they believe fit in each tier of support for both academics and behavior at the school.

Step 3: For each item listed in each tier, see if the stakeholders can identify the who, what, how, and measured for each of the items listed.

Step 4: Use this information to make sure all stakeholders understand what is offered in each tier for both academics and behavior at the school, along with how students and teachers can access the different tiers of support.

Step 5: Complete the Research- or Evidence-Based Practices template (provided in this section) to make sure what is being implemented or offered is evidence based.

Step 5: Create an MTSS pyramid or organizational graphic for your school.

Icon Source: istock.com/appleuzr

MTSS Audit: Menu of Responses, Initiatives, Interventions, Programs

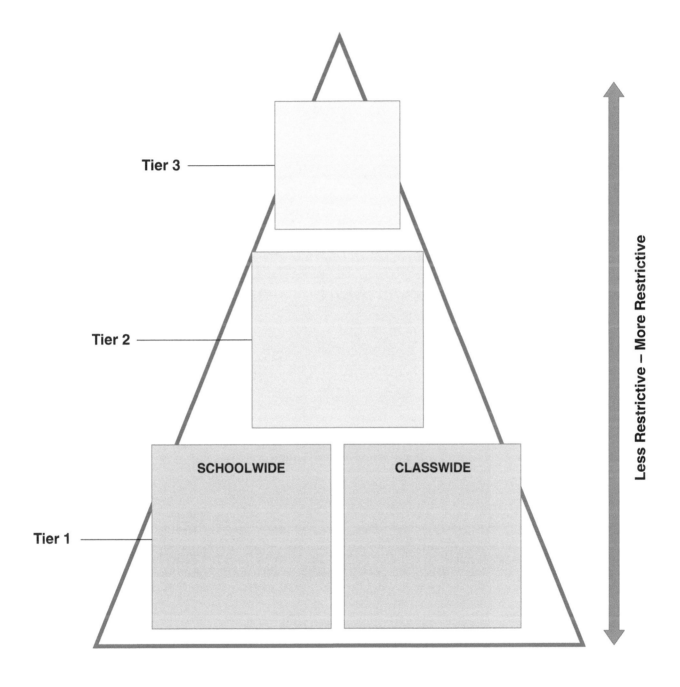

Available for download at resources.corwin.com/MTSSStartupGuide

Research or Evidence-Based Practices template: Behavior/SEL version

PART 1: BEHAVIOR/SEL				
Theory of action: *If we implement a prevention and intervention behavior system . . .*				
Name of the initiative or program	Research	Person(s) responsible	By when	Status
SEL	CASEL			

PART 2: BEHAVIOR/SEL			
Theory of action: *If we implement a prevention and intervention behavior system . . .* Identified initiative: SEL			
Action	Person(s) responsible	By when	Status

PART 3: BEHAVIOR/SEL—INTERIM MEASURE	
Date:	
Theory of action: *If we implement a prevention and intervention behavior system . . .* Identified initiative: SEL	
Adult outcome	Student outcome
All teachers will be trained in SEL core competencies 50% of teachers will be applying SEL core competencies 80% of the time.	50% of students will be observed responding to SEL core competencies based on classroom observations, social and emotional data collection, and student/teacher survey.

online resources   Available for download at resources.corwin.com/MTSSStartupGuide

Research or Evidence–Based Practices template: Academic version

PART 1: ACADEMICS				
Theory of action: *If we implement an engaging curriculum . . .*				
Name of the initiative or program	Research	Person(s) Responsible	By when	Status
UDL	CAST			

PART 2: ACADEMICS			
Theory of action: *If we implement an engaging curriculum . . .* Identified initiative: UDL			
Action	Person(s) responsible	By when	Status

PART 3: ACADEMICS—INTERIM MEASURE	
Date:	
Theory of action: *If we implement an engaging curriculum . . .* Identified initiative: UDL	
Adult outcome	Student outcome
All teachers will be trained in UDL principles. 50% of teachers will be using UDL engagement strategies 80% of the time.	50% of students will be observed responding to UDL engagement strategies based on classroom observations and work samples.

online resources   Available for download at resources.corwin.com/MTSSStartupGuide

Red flags and tips to consider

RED FLAG	TIP TO CONSIDER
The MTSS team does not have a clear understanding of what is offered in each tier and why.	Conduct an audit of all that is offered in the school, and have the stakeholders take part in the audit process and next-steps planning to ensure that everyone is working toward common MTSS schoolwide goals.
The stakeholders do not know how to access each tier.	Make the access points clear for each of the tiers and the supports provided.
The supports in the tiers are not evidence based (i.e., there is no way of knowing if it is working).	Each item provided in the tiered audit has a list of criteria as evidence to measure its effectiveness.
There are no entrance or exit criteria for each tier of support.	Identify entrance and exit criteria for the menu of supports based on data points and student needs.

INDICATOR 4

Commitment for Implementation

Audit current organizational structures and evidence-based practices (i.e., tiered processes/continuum of supports in place, programs, teams, human resources/ expertise/training, initiatives, interventions) for academics and behavior

COMMITMENT	SUCCESS CRITERIA (EVIDENCE OF IMPLEMENTATION)	BY WHOM/WHEN

 Available for download at resources.corwin.com/MTSSStartupGuide

Assess the current state of academic and behavior instruction based on multiple data points

(i.e., data-based problem-solving and decision-making)

 Assess the current state of academic and behavior instruction based on multiple data points (both quantitative and qualitative) for all tiers of support. Have a data-based problem-solving and decision-making process in place that can help all stakeholders begin to identify precise problem statements and possible root causes. Have a process in place to help ensure adequate and timely data are being collected and are available for analysis by the MTSS team representative of each tier.

Success criteria

- ▶ Needed data are identified for both academics and behavior in each tier
- ▶ Both quantitative and qualitative data are utilized
- ▶ Data are updated and available for MTSS meetings
- ▶ Processes are set to ensure accountability of current data
- ▶ All students are represented in the data utilized

Practical tool from the field and implementation process: MTSS Data Organization Sheet

Process for this tool

Step 1: List all the data available for academics and behavior at the school.

Step 2: For each listed item, identify the purpose of the data, how often the data can be retrieved, what stakeholder group the data impact, for what tier of support the data help monitor progress, and what schoolwide MTSS goal the data support.

Icon Source: istock.com/appleuzr

MTSS Data Organization Sheet

What data are needed for our MTSS meetings? quantitative and qualitative? For what MTSS schoolwide goal will the data help monitor progress?	Who is responsible?

Sample quantitative and qualitative data points available at a school

QUANTITATIVE DATA EXAMPLE	QUALITATIVE DATA EXAMPLE
Demographics, ethnicity, gender, school characteristics	Interviews, observations, climate surveys (open-ended)
Teacher and specialist qualifications	Classroom environment visits, visuals, celebrations
Student performance, promotion rates, grades, advanced placement scores	MTSS descriptions (criteria for entrance and exit)
Drop-out rates	Stakeholder focus groups (students, staff, community)
Student engagement, attendance, school involvement	Discipline practice and process descriptions
Suspensions, detentions, expulsions	Intervention referral practice and process descriptions
Culture and climate survey (students, staff, community)	Evidence of UDL
Social and emotional interventions and programs offered	Mission/vision/values/beliefs
Number of students receiving SPED services	Clear school SMART goals (academic and behavior)
Number of students receiving 504 accommodations	School site plan
Number of students on individualized behavior/SEL supports	Local control accountability plan

Source: Hannigan and Hannigan (2019).

Screener data suggestions

EXAMPLES OF POSSIBLE ASSESSMENTS/SCREENERS ALL STUDENTS CAN COMPLETE	
ASSESSMENTS	OTHER
State assessments	Curriculum-based measures
State aligned benchmark assessments	Fluency measures
Teacher team–created assessments	Behavior
	Grade point average
	Attendance
	School connectedness
	School safety measures
	Past curriculum measures
	Program or intervention: baseline assessments
	SEL screeners
	Teacher team–created screeners

Red flags and tips to consider

RED FLAG	TIP TO CONSIDER
Data are not utilized during MTSS meetings or action planning.	Establish a process to make sure all data points are aligned with the schoolwide MTSS goals so that there is a check-in on everyone's updated data toward these goals at every meeting.
Only quantitative measures are utilized.	Use qualitative data points as well, such as perception data, student voice, observations, and interviews (i.e., empathy interviews).
Some members frequently do not have updated data to support their claims.	If there is a problem with data collection, provide support to the lead responsible for those data.
The leadership does not hold accountability for all those involved in data collection.	Members are held accountable for updated and timely data. Meetings and decisions are not based on emotion but data.

INDICATOR 5

Commitment for Implementation

Assess the current state of academic and behavior instruction based on multiple data points (i.e., data-based problem-solving and decision-making)		
COMMITMENT	**SUCCESS CRITERIA (EVIDENCE OF IMPLEMENTATION)**	**BY WHOM/WHEN**

 Available for download at resources.corwin.com/MTSSStartupGuide

Develop and share MTSS SMART goals and actions for academics and behavior

INDICATOR #6

(i.e., based on assessment, screener, trend, qualitative, and quantitative data)

The MTSS team creates a schoolwide goal (less is more) for academics and behavior implementation. Every grade-level or department team sets their goals in alignment with schoolwide and district goals and understands their role in helping attain them. There is a plan that exists to monitor a team's progress toward the SMART goals. The goals provide a target that allows teams to celebrate and/or reflect on their progress by answering "why" or "why not."

Much in the same way that relevant and timely feedback is essential for a student's progress toward learning at high levels, relevant and timely feedback needs to be communicated for a *team's* progress toward its goals.

Success criteria

▶ MTSS team creates schoolwide goals (i.e., at least one schoolwide academic goal and one schoolwide behavior goal)

▶ All stakeholders contribute to goal development

▶ Progress-monitoring structures are in place for every goal

▶ Short-term and long-term goal attainments are celebrated and shared with all stakeholders

▶ Process for relevant and timely feedback needs to be communicated for a team's progress toward its goals

▶ Completed MTSS Planning Guide (template provided in this section)

Practical tool from the field and implementation process: MTSS Planning Guide: Schoolwide Version

Process for this tool

Step 1: With the MTSS team, complete the MTSS Planning Guide: Schoolwide Version.

Step 2: As a team, discuss any questions and/or concerns.

Step 3: Utilize the planning guide to keep your implementation focused, aligned, and coordinated at every meeting.

Icon Source: istock.com/appleuzr

MTSS Planning Guide: Schoolwide Version

WHY DO WE EXIST (PURPOSE)?
Schoolwide mission:
MTSS team mission:
Beliefs/values/perceptions:
Scheduled MTSS meeting dates:
Accountability measures (i.e., school, district, state, local education agency, and federal levels):
MTSS team member roles/responsibilities:
Other stakeholders (i.e., community, families, partnerships, etc.):
Current state of the school (where are we now?):
Contributing factors (how did we get to where we are—successes and challenges?):
How do we know if what we are doing is working? How will we implement it?
School processes: *What initiatives (frameworks, programs, instructional, organizational, leadership, continuous improvement, etc.) will be implemented?*
Where do we want to be? Student learning? Student behavior? School culture?
Academic initiative implementation objective(s):
Behavior initiative implementation objective(s):

MTSS SMART GOALS

MTSS long-term schoolwide SMART Goal 1:

Baseline:

Long-term schoolwide SMART goal proficiency measures:

Data (measures of proficiency—quantitative and qualitative):

MTSS QUARTERLY SMART GOAL 1 PROGRESS MONITORING

SMART GOAL 1 Quarter 1:	SMART GOAL 1 Quarter 2:	SMART GOAL 1 Quarter 3:	SMART GOAL 1 Quarter 4:
Measure of proficiency:	Measure of proficiency:	Measure of proficiency:	Measure of proficiency:

MTSS QUARTERLY SMART GOAL 1 PRIORITY ACTIONS

Priority actions	By when/by whom	Funding/policy/resources necessary
Action 1		
Action 2		
Action 3		

(Continued)

(Continued)

MTSS long-term schoolwide SMART Goal 2:			
Baseline:			
Long-term schoolwide SMART goal proficiency measures:			
Data (measures of proficiency):			

MTSS QUARTERLY SMART GOAL 2 PROGRESS MONITORING

SMART GOAL 2 Quarter 1:	SMART GOAL 2 Quarter 2:	SMART GOAL 2 Quarter 3:	SMART GOAL 2 Quarter 4:
Measure of proficiency:	Measure of proficiency:	Measure of proficiency:	Measure of proficiency:

MTSS QUARTERLY SMART GOAL 2 PRIORITY ACTIONS

Priority actions	By when/by whom	Funding/policy/resources necessary
Action 1		
Action 2		
Action 3		

MTSS long-term schoolwide SMART Goal 3:

Baseline:

Long-term schoolwide SMART goal proficiency measures:

Data (measures of proficiency):

MTSS QUARTERLY SMART GOAL 3 PROGRESS MONITORING

SMART GOAL 3 Quarter 1:	SMART GOAL 3 Quarter 2:	SMART GOAL 3 Quarter 3:	SMART GOAL 3 Quarter 4:
Measure of proficiency:	Measure of proficiency:	Measure of proficiency:	Measure of proficiency:

MTSS QUARTERLY SMART GOAL 3 PRIORITY ACTIONS

Priority actions	By when/by whom	Funding/policy/resources necessary
Action 1		
Action 2		
Action 3		

(Continued)

(Continued)

MTSS long-term schoolwide SMART Goal 4:
Baseline:
Long-term schoolwide SMART goal proficiency measures:
Data (measures of proficiency):

MTSS QUARTERLY SMART GOAL 4 PROGRESS MONITORING			
SMART GOAL 4 Quarter 1:	SMART GOAL 4 Quarter 2:	SMART GOAL 4 Quarter 3:	SMART GOAL 4 Quarter 4:
Measure of proficiency:	Measure of proficiency:	Measure of proficiency:	Measure of proficiency:

MTSS QUARTERLY SMART GOAL 4 PRIORITY ACTIONS		
Priority actions	By when/by whom	Funding/policy/resources necessary
Action 1		
Action 2		
Action 3		

Additional factors to consider (discussion/decision/task—if applicable):

ADMINISTRATIVE LEADERSHIP	INTEGRATED EDUCATIONAL FRAMEWORK	FAMILY AND COMMUNITY ENGAGEMENT	INCLUSIVE POLICY STRUCTURE AND PRACTICE

SMART goal behavior/SEL template

SMART GOAL CHARACTERISTICS	OUR SCHOOLWIDE BEHAVIOR/SEL GOAL: *WRITE YOUR SCHOOLWIDE BEHAVIOR GOAL*
Strategic and **S**pecific	*Write the portion of your schoolwide behavior goal evidencing that it is strategic and specific.*
Measurable	*Write the portion of your schoolwide behavior goal evidencing that it is measurable.*
Attainable/**A**chievable	*Explain why you believe your schoolwide behavior goal is attainable or achievable.*
Results Oriented and **R**elevant	*Write the portion of your schoolwide behavior goal evidencing that it is results oriented and relevant.*
Time Bound	*Write the portion of your schoolwide behavior goal evidencing that it is time bound.*

online resources ↘ Available for download at resources.corwin.com/MTSSStartupGuide

SMART goal academic template

SMART GOAL CHARACTERISTICS	OUR SCHOOLWIDE ACADEMIC GOAL: *WRITE YOUR SCHOOLWIDE ACADEMIC GOAL*
Strategic and **S**pecific	*Write the portion of your schoolwide academic goal evidencing that it is strategic and specific.*
Measurable	*Write the portion of your schoolwide academic goal evidencing that it is measurable.*
Attainable/**A**chievable	*Explain why you believe your schoolwide academic goal is attainable/achievable.*
Results Oriented and **R**elevant	*Write the portion of your schoolwide academic goal evidencing that it is results oriented and relevant.*
Time Bound	*Write the portion of your schoolwide academic goal evidencing that it is time bound.*

online resources Available for download at resources.corwin.com/MTSSStartupGuide

Red flags and tips to consider

RED FLAG	TIP TO CONSIDER
No schoolwide goals are set for academics and behavior.	Gather stakeholder input and conduct a data analysis to help your team develop schoolwide academic and behavior goals.
There are some goals set, but they are not SMART.	Make sure all goals follow the SMART criteria.
Goals are too narrow.	Your team can reach its SMART goal while not requiring students to learn at high levels.
Stakeholders do not know the goals.	Educate all stakeholders on the goals.
Progress monitoring is not in place.	Set up progress-monitoring measures for the goals.
Celebration of goals is not evident.	Create opportunities for goal attainment celebration with all stakeholders.

INDICATOR 6

Commitment for Implementation

Develop and share MTSS SMART goals and actions for academics and behavior (i.e., based on assessment, screener, trend, qualitative, and quantitative data)		
COMMITMENT	SUCCESS CRITERIA (EVIDENCE OF IMPLEMENTATION)	BY WHOM/BY WHEN

Set up a progress-monitoring system/benchmarks for MTSS, and ensure that assessment and data are up-to-date and available for decision-making

The MTSS team has a process for progress monitoring MTSS implementation and benchmark goals for academics and behavior in each tier by utilizing data for decision-making and problem-solving.

Success criteria

▶ MTSS Team Agenda completed at least monthly

▶ Problem statements and next-step actions based on tiers articulated in documents

▶ Evidence of implementation of the actions for each tier

▶ Share-out process with key stakeholders

Practical tool from the field and implementation process: MTSS Team Agenda

Process for this tool

Step 1: Familiarize yourself and all MTSS team members with the agenda format.

Step 2: Assign roles to ensure the agenda is filled out.

Step 3: Utilize the agenda during MTSS team meetings—meeting memory and progress-monitoring checks embedded into the agenda.

Step 4: Share out the agenda with appropriate stakeholders—decide as a team what is appropriate for sharing information with your stakeholders.

MTSS Team Agenda template

Today's meeting date/time:	Location:	Facilitator:	Minutes taker:	Timekeeper:	Data keeper:
Next meeting date/time:	Location:	Facilitator:	Minutes taker:	Timekeeper:	Data keeper:

MTSS TEAM MEMBERS (BOLD WHO IS PRESENT)

MTSS TEAM GUIDING QUESTIONS

Who are we? What is our purpose?
What is our current state? How did we get here?
Is what we are doing making a difference academically, behaviorally, and socio-emotionally for our students?
Where do we want to be? How will we get there?
How will we respond if we are not progressing toward our goals? How will we utilize data to help us make decisions?

MTSS TEAM GUIDING QUESTIONS

TODAY'S AGENDA ITEMS (OUTCOMES)	NEXT MEETING AGENDA ITEMS (OUTCOMES)—POTENTIAL PROBLEMS RAISED

SCHOOLWIDE MTSS SMART GOALS

Tiered Systems of Support at a glance	Data Check (How are we doing in support for our schoolwide MTSS SMART goals?)	Precise problem statement based on review of the data (Who, What, Where, When, Why)	Solution actions (decision rules)	By Whom/ When? Resources needed?	Communication to all stakeholders? Who? What? When?
Tier 1 Academics					
Tier 2 Academics					
Tier 3 Academics					
Tier 1 Behavior/SEL					
Tier 2 Behavior/SEL					
Tier 3 Behavior/SEL					

online resources   Available for download at resources.corwin.com/MTSSStartupGuide

ADMINISTRATIVE LEADERSHIP, INTEGRATED EDUCATIONAL FRAMEWORK, FAMILY AND COMMUNITY ENGAGEMENT, INCLUSIVE POLICY STRUCTURE AND PRACTICE			
Information for team, stakeholder input, or issue for team to address (policy, implementation fidelity, budget/funding, leadership)	Discussion/decision/task (if applicable)	By whom?	When?

Red flags and tips to consider

RED FLAG	TIP TO CONSIDER
MTSS meetings are not structured and focused.	Make sure the MTSS meetings are focused around the overall schoolwide goals.
MTSS teams do not cover all the necessary areas.	Designate a member to ensure that every member has a voice.
Data are not utilized and logged to help with progress monitoring of actions and next steps.	Data points and aims need to be logged and revisited at every meeting.
MTSS team meetings are too overwhelming.	Stay focused on the agenda items.
Some members hijack the MTSS team meeting time.	Allocate adequate time for each tier of support data share out and next steps.

INDICATOR 7

Commitment for Implementation

Set up a progress-monitoring system/benchmarks for MTSS, and ensure that assessment and data are up-to-date and available for decision-making		
COMMITMENT	SUCCESS CRITERIA (EVIDENCE OF IMPLEMENTATION)	BY WHOM/WHEN

INDICATOR #8

Set up clear communication structures between the MTSS team and all stakeholders

There are clear communication structures or flowcharts set up between the MTSS team members and all stakeholders. Ongoing opportunities are provided for all stakeholders to communicate their needs and concerns, and feedback or responses are timely.

Success criteria

▶ Designee from the MTSS team is the lead on communication from the meetings (at least monthly)

▶ Staff meetings have an embedded MTSS time for communication and sharing opportunities

▶ The MTSS agendas are transparent and accessible

▶ Stakeholders have an opportunity to contribute to MTSS agenda items

▶ There are safe structures in place for all stakeholders to provide information to the MTSS team at all times

Practical tool from the field and implementation process: MTSS Team Communication Structure

Process for this tool

Step 1: With the MTSS team, flowchart the communication process from the MTSS team to other staff not on the team.

Step 2: With the MTSS team, flowchart the opportunities a stakeholder at the school has to provide ongoing input.

Step 3: With the MTSS team, flowchart how a stakeholder not on the school campus can provide input.

Step 4: Identify areas where communication can improve within the system of support; share suggestions for improvement with stakeholders, collect their input, and put commitments in place to improve ongoing communication.

Sample MTSS Team Communication Structure between MTSS team members and all staff members

Staff agenda item:		
STAFF AGENDA FIXED ITEM	TIME	OUTCOME
MTSS focus	*3:00–3:45*	*Stakeholder input and role clarification*

Additional ideas for communication

- ❑ Memo from the MTSS team after each meeting (at least monthly)
- ❑ Link provided to MTSS agendas (transparency)
- ❑ Link provided to all staff to discuss anonymous MTSS input/questions/suggestions/issues/needs, and so on
- ❑ Student input link

Red flags and tips to consider

RED FLAG	TIP TO CONSIDER
Stakeholders have lost trust in the MTSS team because what they communicate and what actually gets implemented do not match.	Make sure the actions decided by the MTSS team are implemented.
Communication is not timely.	Share MTSS information 1–3 days after the MTSS team meeting. A best practice is to make the agenda available to all and have a process in place for all stakeholders to have an opportunity to provide input for the agenda.
Stakeholders do not feel as if they are heard.	Provide safe opportunities for all stakeholders to give input on what is working or not working.
Lack of transparency in the decisions made by the MTSS team.	Make the MTSS agenda and notes transparent. Be mindful about posting any individual student information. Use professional judgment.

INDICATOR 8

Commitment for Implementation

Set up clear communication structures between the MTSS team and all stakeholders		
COMMITMENT	SUCCESS CRITERIA (EVIDENCE OF IMPLEMENTATION)	BY WHOM/WHEN

 Available for download at resources.corwin.com/MTSSStartupGuide

Set up ongoing MTSS professional learning for all stakeholders

INDICATOR
#9

The MTSS team designs an ongoing professional learning structure through a variety of modalities, with opportunities for learning based on stakeholder group needs. This may include in person, online, shorter refreshers, and booster session quarterly for all stakeholder groups. Structures for professional learning are set up for new school staff and stakeholders to participate in MTSS learning opportunities.

Success criteria

- MTSS professional learning calendar is set and available to all stakeholders (includes quarterly training opportunities for all stakeholder groups), with room for adjustments as needed based on stakeholder needs
- There is internal capacity building within the MTSS team to provide ongoing professional learning and support
- Multiple modalities of professional learning are provided (in person or online)
- Funding is allocated toward professional opportunities for all stakeholders

Practical tool from the field and implementation process: MTSS Training Schedule

Process for this tool

Step 1: As an MTSS team, assess the professional learning needs of all stakeholders.

Step 2: Develop a draft calendar of MTSS professional learning opportunities (quarterly for all groups).

Step 3: Designate a lead from the MTSS team to ensure that professional learning opportunities are in place.

Step 4: Share the professional learning calendar with all stakeholder groups.

Icon Source: istock.com/appleuzr

Sample MTSS Training Schedule

AUGUST MTSS TRAINING TOPICS	STAKEHOLDER GROUP	OUTCOME	BY WHOM/WHEN
Roles/responsibilities of the MTSS team	*School MTSS team*	*The MTSS team members understand MTSS and develop their purpose based on stakeholder input*	*Designated district office MTSS expert* *(By August 1)*
What is MTSS?	*School staff*	*The school staff understand MTSS and develop a shared responsibility for the work*	*Designated district office MTSS expert and school site MTSS team members* *(By August 25)*
Parents and community members' role in MTSS implementation	*Parents and community*	*Stakeholders understand MTSS and how they can collaborate with the school*	*Designated MTSS team members* *(By August 25)*

MTSS Training Schedule template

AUGUST MTSS TRAINING TOPICS	STAKEHOLDER GROUP	OUTCOME	BY WHOM/WHEN

online resources 🔎 Available for download at resources.corwin.com/MTSSStartupGuide

Red flags and tips to consider

RED FLAG	TIP TO CONSIDER
MTSS professional learning opportunities are not relatable to all stakeholders.	Have someone who has implemented, has trained to implement, and/or understands tiered systems provide the training. Gauge the need from the stakeholder group prior to presenting the learning so the professional learning opportunity meets their needs.
MTSS professional learning opportunities are not provided on a regular basis—usually only at the beginning of the school year.	Professional learning opportunities are provided regularly, with multiple modalities that allow groups access to the content. This provides all members of the group opportunities to still learn together even if all members are not present.
There is no structure set for new stakeholders, such as teachers and staff new to the school.	Designate a component of new staff orientation for MTSS development.
There is a lack of funding for professional learning opportunities.	Allocate resources to reflect this work as a priority on your campus. To have a better chance at receiving support from stakeholders, demonstrate how these opportunities are building a strong MTSS foundation at your school toward focused goals.

INDICATOR 9

Commitment for Implementation

Set up ongoing MTSS professional learning for all stakeholders		
COMMITMENT	SUCCESS CRITERIA (EVIDENCE OF IMPLEMENTATION)	BY WHOM/WHEN

online resources   Available for download at resources.corwin.com/MTSSStartupGuide

Set up a process for ongoing evaluation and continuous improvement of MTSS implementation effectiveness and fidelity

INDICATOR #10

 MTSS team members have agreed on a process they utilize to help them stay accountable for the MTSS implementation work.

Success criteria

▶ There is an accountability structure in place for MTSS implementation (norms, collective agreements)

▶ All MTSS members understand and agree on the evaluation and continuous-improvement process

▶ Implementation fidelity checks are in place at least quarterly

Practical tool from the field and implementation process: School-at-a-Glance Improvement Tool

Process for this tool

Step 1: As an MTSS team, identify a focus area (academic or social well-being) need of the school based on data; insert the focus area at the top of the template.

Step 2: After identifying a focus area, work through each of the prompts, starting at the bottom of the template structure (use the completed sample as a reference).

Step 3: Develop a precise problem statement as a team. Take the precise problem statement through a vetting process to identify contributing factors and/or root causes (i.e., structural factors are often written rules or policy schedules, and institutional factors are often the unwritten beliefs and behaviors of stakeholders: "This is how we have always done it").

Step 4: Go through the plan, do, study, act stages as a team based on all of this information. This template is designed to assist in this ongoing continuous school improvement process and incorporates common key components of effective continuous-improvement models.

Note: An MTSS team can have a few of these school-at-a-glance improvement templates going concurrently that are revisited at each MTSS team meeting. We have found this to be a less overwhelming and good visual process for team members.

Icon Source: istock.com/appleuzr

School-at-a-Glance Improvement Tool

Focus Area: Inclusion of Students With Disabilities (disability category—reading)

PLAN
- Review current ELA inclusion schedules and provided services/supports of the identified 15 students.
- Bring together the SPED and ELA general education teachers to develop a schedule for inclusion during core ELA instruction for the identified 15 students.

DO
- Implement the ELA inclusion schedules for all 15 students for 2–3 weeks.
- Provide SPED push in support during core ELA instruction for 2–3 weeks.

STUDY
- Monitor and measure effectiveness of ELA inclusion schedule with proper SPED supports around grade-level common assessments, teacher perception data after 2–3 weeks.

ACT
- Ensure schedules are being implemented with fidelity.
- SPED teachers push in to ELA grade-level teacher team meetings to work together on providing needed supports for the 15 students.

Contributing Factors (Structural)
- SPED pull-out schedule
- IEP language/minutes
- Number of SPED students being served at the school
- RTI/PLC not in place

Contributing Factors (Institutional)
- General education teacher beliefs and perceptions that students with disabilities should be served by SPED teachers only—"We have always done it that way" trend identified.

Precise Problem Statement
Students with disabilities, specifically with an identified learning disability in the area of reading, are not meeting ELA standards based on state, district, and grade-level ELA assessments for the past 3 years. Out of 15 students identified, 0% have met mastery. In addition, on average, these students are pulled out during core ELA instruction.

Mission, Vision, Target (Desired State)
Mission: Ensure all students will succeed academically, socially, and emotionally.
Target (Desired State): Students with disabilities (with an identified disability in the area of reading) at School A are effectively included in their general education classroom settings during core ELA instruction (7–7th grade, 8–8th grade students).

Note: ELA, English language arts; IEP, Individualized Education Program.

School-at-a-Glance Improvement Tool template

Focus Area: _____

PLAN

- _____
- _____
- _____
- _____

DO

- _____
- _____
- _____
- _____

STUDY

- _____
- _____

ACT

- _____
- _____

Contributing Factors (Structural)

- _____
- _____
- _____
- _____

Contributing Factors (Institutional)

- _____
- _____
- _____
- _____

Precise Problem Statement

_____
_____
_____
_____

Mission, Vision, Target (Desired State)

_____
_____
_____
_____

Red flags and tips to consider

RED FLAG	TIP TO CONSIDER
No consistent continuous-improvement process in place	Research as a team, and decide what is the best fit for the MTSS team
The MTSS team does not understand the continuous-improvement process	Provide training and practice for utilizing the continuous-improvement process as a team
No MTSS evaluation structures in place	Set up MTSS evaluation structures for all 10 indicators in this book. Intentionally revisit them at least three times a year

INDICATOR 10

Commitment for Implementation

Set up a process for ongoing evaluation and continuous improvement of MTSS implementation effectiveness and fidelity		
COMMITMENT	SUCCESS CRITERIA (EVIDENCE OF IMPLEMENTATION)	BY WHOM/WHEN

online resources

Available for download at resources.corwin.com/MTSSStartupGuide

PART IV

BRINGING IT ALL TOGETHER

CHAPTER 6

BRINGING IT ALL TOGETHER

Now that you and your team have processed through the 10 indicators, take some time to bring it all together in this action plan template. Revisit this action plan on a regular basis as you meet as a team, to ensure that you are staying on track with your commitments.

MTSS START-UP ACTION PLAN			
Indicator	Priority next steps	By whom/when	Status/evidence
Indicator 1: Establish an MTSS team (i.e., team-driven and shared leadership)			
Indicator 2: Assess stakeholder beliefs, perceptions, shared values, and identity, and establish the mission and purpose of the MTSS team and all stakeholders (i.e., families, school, community, partnerships, etc.)			
Indicator 3: Establish and apportion roles and responsibilities among MTSS team members and all stakeholders (i.e., shared ownership and responsibility)			
Indicator 4: Audit current organizational structures and evidence-based practices (i.e., tiered processes/continuum of supports in place, programs, teams, human resources/expertise/training, initiatives, interventions) for academics and behavior			

Indicator	Priority next steps	By whom/when	Status/evidence
Indicator 5: Assess the current state of academic and behavior instruction based on multiple data points (i.e., data-based problem-solving and decision-making)			
Indicator 6: Develop and share MTSS SMART goals and actions for academics and behavior (i.e., based on assessment, screener, trend, qualitative, and quantitative data)			
Indicator 7: Set up a progress-monitoring system/benchmarks for MTSS, and ensure that assessment and data are up-to-date and available for decision-making			
Indicator 8: Set up clear communication structures between the MTSS team and all stakeholders			
Indicator 9: Set up ongoing MTSS professional learning for all stakeholders			
Indicator 10: Set up a process for ongoing evaluation and continuous improvement of MTSS implementation effectiveness and fidelity			

NOTES

_____

_____

_____

_____

_____

_____

_____

_____

online resources   Available for download at resources.corwin.com/MTSSStartupGuide.

Thank you for beginning this journey with us. Focus on one indicator at a time. Soon the outcomes from each of the indicators will build on one another to create a strong model MTSS foundation designed to help *all* students succeed in your school. Before you go, write down your commitment to this work, sign, and note down the date for your records.

I commit to implementing the MTSS starting actions by . . .

_____

_____

_____

_____

_____

Signature _____

Date _____

REFERENCES

Bolman, L. G., & Deal, T. E. (2007). *Reframing organizations: Artistry, choice, and leadership.* Jossey-Bass.

Buffum, A., Mattos, M., & Weber, C. A. (2012). *Simplifying response to intervention: Four essential guiding principles.* Solution Tree Press.

Buffum, A. G., Mattos, M. W., & Malone, J. (2018). *Taking action: A handbook for RTI at Work.* Solution Tree Press.

DuFour, R., DuFour, R., Eaker, R., Many, T. W., & Mattos, M. (2016). *Learning by doing: A handbook for professional learning communities at work* (3rd ed.). Solution Tree Australia.

Hannigan, J. D., & Hannigan, J. (2019). *Building behavior: The educator's guide to evidence-based initiatives.* Corwin. https://doi.org/10.4135/9781071800492

Mattos, M., & Buffum, A. (Eds.). (2015). *It's about time: Planning interventions and extensions in secondary school.* Solution Tree Press.

Further Readings

Abdulla Badri, M., Selim, H., Alshare, K., Grandon, E., Younis, H., & Abdulla, M. (2006). The Baldrige Education Criteria for Performance Excellence Framework: Empirical test and validation. *International Journal of Quality & Reliability Management, 23*(9), 1118–1157. https://doi.org/10.1108/02656710610704249

Bryk, A. S. (2018). *Advancing quality in continuous improvement* [Speech presentation]. The Carnegie Foundation Summit on Improvement in Education, San Francisco, CA, United States.

Deming, W. E. (2014). *PDSA cycle.* W. Edwards Deming Institute. https://deming.org/explore/p-d-s-a#

Fixsen, D., Blase, K. A., Metz, A., & Van Dyke, M. (2015). Implementation science. In J. D. Wright (Ed.), *International encyclopedia of the social and behavioral sciences* (2nd ed., Vol. 11, pp. 695–702). Elsevier. https://doi.org/10.1016/B978-0-08-097086-8.10548-3

Hannigan, J., & Hauser, L. (2015). *The PBIS Tier One handbook: A practical approach to implementing the champion model.* Corwin.

Hannigan, J. D., & Hannigan, J. (2018a). *The PBIS Tier Two handbook: A practical approach to implementing the champion model.* Corwin.

Hannigan, J. D., & Hannigan, J. (2018b). *The PBIS Tier Three handbook: A practical approach to implementing the champion model.* Corwin.

Langley, G. J., Moen, R. D., Nolan, K. M., Nolan, T. W., Norman, C. L., & Provost, L. P. (2009). *The improvement guide: A practical approach to enhancing organizational performance.* John Wiley & Sons.

Lewis, C. (2015). What is improvement science? Do we need it in education? *Educational Researcher, 44*(1), 54–61. https://doi.org/10.3102/0013189X15570388

Louison, L., & Fleming, O. (2017). *Context matters: Recommendations for funders and program developers supporting implementation in rural communities.* National Implementation Science Network.

Novak, K. (2014). *UDL now! A teacher's Monday-morning guide to implementing Common Core Standards using Universal Design Learning.* CAST Professional.

Sugai, G., & Horner, R. R. (2006). A promising approach for expanding and sustaining school-wide positive behavior support. *School Psychology Review, 35*(2), 245–259. https://www.icareby.org/sites/www.icareby.org/files/spr352sugai.pdf

Taylor, R. D., Oberle, E., Durlak, J. A., & Weissberg, R. P. (2017). Promoting positive youth development through school-based Social and Emotional Learning interventions: A meta-analysis of follow-up effects. *Child Development, 88*(4), 1156–1171. https://doi.org/10.1111/cdev.12864

INDEX

Agenda, MTSS Team, 75–77
Audit, MTSS
   Menu of Responses, Initiatives, Interventions,
      Programs, 53
   Roles and Responsibilities, 41–49

Bolman, L. G., 2
Buffum, A., 9, 11

Common Core State Standards, 8
Communication structures, 80–82
Continuous-improvement process, 87–91
Culturally responsive teaching, 9, 11

Data assessment, 58–62
Data-based problem-solving, 58–62
Data Organization Sheet, MTSS, 59
Deal, T. E., 2
Decision-making, 58–62, 74–79
   student voice in, 11
District-led school, 12–13

80/15/5 rule, 11
Enrichment opportunities, 10
Everything Everything School, 12
Evidence-based practices, 52–57
Extension opportunities, 10

Gifted and Talented Education, 10
Grouping students, 10

Identification strategies, 11

Kindergarten, 11

Labeling, 10

Mattos, M., 9
Menu of Responses, Initiatives, Interventions,
   Programs, 53
MTSS
   approaches, 9
   Audit. *See* Audit, MTSS
   Data Organization Sheet, 59
   defined, 2
   in district-led school, 12–13

   in Everything Everything School, 12
   Gifted and Talented Education in, 10
   goal of, 4
   Model, 4, 9
   PBIS *versus*, 8
   Planning Guide, 64–69
   purpose, 2
   Readiness Screener, 16–18
   RTI *versus*, 8–9
   in site-led school, 13
   Start-Up Assessment, 18–21
   student voice in, 11, 30
   subteams, 4
   team. *See* Team, MTSS
   Training Schedule, 84
   transitional kindergarten/kindergarten, 11
   UDL in, 9
MTSS implementation, 5, 23–24, 94–95
   academic and behavior data assessment, 58–62
   communication structures, 80–82
   continuous-improvement process, 87–91
   effectiveness and fidelity, 87–91
   evidence-based practices, 52–57
   MTSS team establishment, 25–29
   MTSS team mission/vision establishment, 30–39
   organizational structures, auditing, 52–57
   professional learning, setting up, 83–86
   progress monitoring system/benchmarks for,
      74–79
   roles and responsibilities, 40–51
   SMART goals, 63–73
Multi-Tiered Systems of Support (MTSS). *See* MTSS

Ongoing professional learning, 83–86
Organizational structures, auditing, 52–57
Organizational theory, 2
Organization Prompt, MTSS Team, 26, 27

PBIS. *See* Positive Behavior Interventions and
   Supports (PBIS)
Planning Guide, MTSS, 64–69
PLC. *See* Professional Learning Communities (PLC)
Positive Behavior Interventions and
   Supports (PBIS)
   MTSS *versus*, 8
   at Work, 4

Precise problem statement, 87
Problem-solving, data-based, 58–62
Professional learning, 83–86
Professional Learning Communities (PLC), 4
Progress monitoring system, 74–79

Qualitative and quantitative data, 60

Readiness Screener, MTSS, 16–18
Reframing Organizations (Bolman & Deal), 2
Research-based practices, 52–57
Response to Intervention (RTI), 3
    MTSS *versus*, 8–9
    SPED and, 9–10
    at Work, 4, 9
Restorative practices, 11
Roles and responsibilities, 40–51
RTI. *See* Response to Intervention (RTI)

School-at-a-Glance Improvement Tool, 88–89
School Collective Commitments Form, 31–33
Schoolwide Roadmap Visual of Collective
        Commitments, 34–35
Screener data, 60
SEL. *See* Social and Emotional Learning (SEL)
Shared leadership, 25–29
Shared ownership, 40–51
Silos, 2
Site-led school, 13
SMART goals, MTSS, 63–73
Social and Emotional Learning (SEL), 4
Special education (SPED)
    RTI and, 9–10
    Tier 3 for, 9–10
Stakeholder(s)
    communication structures between MTSS
        team and, 80–82
    Identification and Action-Planning Form, 36–37

MTSS team mission/vision establishment
        based on feedback of, 30–39
    professional learning for, 83–86
    roles and responsibilities, 40–51
    in silos, 2
Start-Up Assessment, MTSS, 18–21
Student voice in MTSS, 11, 30
Subteams, MTSS, 4
Systematic interventions, 11

Team-driven leadership, 25–29
Team, MTSS
    Agenda, 75–77
    communication structures, 80–82
    establishment, 25–29
    mission/vision establishment, 30–39
    Organization Prompt, 26, 27
    roles and responsibilities, 40–51
    See also MTSS; MTSS implementation
Templates
    evidence-based practices, 54–55
    MTSS Audit: Roles and Responsibilities, 49
    MTSS Team Agenda, 75–77
    MTSS Team Organization Prompt, 27
    MTSS Training Schedule, 84
    School-at-a-Glance Improvement Tool, 89
    School Collective Commitments Form,
        32–33
    Schoolwide Roadmap Visual of Collective
        Commitments, 35
    SMART goal, 70–71
Training Schedule, MTSS, 84
Transitional kindergarten, 11
Trauma-informed practices, 9

Universal Design for Learning (UDL), 4
    defined, 9
    implementation, 9

CORWIN
A SAGE Publishing Company

Helping educators make the greatest impact

CORWIN HAS ONE MISSION: to enhance education through intentional professional learning.

We build long-term relationships with our authors, educators, clients, and associations who partner with us to develop and continuously improve the best evidence-based practices that establish and support lifelong learning.